ABO

Moustafa Gadalla ... graduated from Cairo University with a Bachelor of Science degree in civil engineering in 1967. He immigrated to the U.S.A. in 1971 to practice as a licensed professional engineer and land surveyor.

From his early childhood, Gadalla pursued his Ancient Egyptian roots with passion, through continuous study and research. Since 1990, he has dedicated and concentrated all his time to researching the Ancient Egyptian civilization. As an independent Egyptologist, he spends a part of every year visiting and studying sites of antiquities.

Gadalla is the author of ten internationally acclaimed books. He is the chairman of the Tehuti Research Foundation—an international, U.S.-based, non-profit organization, dedicated to Ancient Egyptian studies.

OTHER BOOKS BY THE AUTHOR

[See details on pages 189-192]

Egyptian Cosmology: The Animated Universe - 2nd ed.

Egyptian Divinities: The All Who Are THE ONE

Egyptian Harmony: The Visual Music

Historical Deception: The Untold Story of Ancient Egypt - 2nd ed.

Egyptian Rhythm: The Heavenly Melodies

Exiled Egyptians: The Heart of Africa

Pyramid Handbook - 2nd ed.

Tut-Ankh-Amen: The Living Image of the Lord

Egypt: A Practical Guide

This Book is Dedicated to

Ka-Anbu
The Guide Within

Book Production by: Moustafa Gadalla and Faith Cross
Book Cover Artwork by: K&D Design, North East, PA, USA

Egyptian Mystics

Seekers of The Way

Moustafa Gadalla
Maa Kheru (True of Voice)

Tehuti Research Foundation
International Head Office: Greensboro, NC, U.S.A.

Egyptian Mystics
Seekers of The Way
by Moustafa Gadalla

Published by:
Tehuti Research Foundation
P.O. Box 39406
Greensboro, NC   27438-9406, U.S.A.

Publisher's Cataloging-in-Publication
(Provided by Quality Books, Inc.)

Gadalla, Moustafa, 1944-
    Egyptian mystics : seekers of the way / Moustafa Gadalla.
    p. cm.
    Includes bibliographical references and index.
    LCCN 2003090012
    ISBN 1-931446-05-9
    ISBN 1-931446-15-6 (E-book)

    1. Sufism--Origin. 2. Sufism--Egypt. 3. Egypt--Religion--Influence. I. Title

BP189.2.G33 2003   297.4
                              QBI03-200038

Manufactured in the United States of America
Published 2003

Table of Contents

I The Hidden Treasure

II Transformation from Dust to Gold

❚❚❚ The Public Visitation Fairs

IIII Come One Come All

Appendices

Preface

Herodotus stated in 500 BCE, *"Of all the nations in the world, the Egyptians are the happiest, healthiest and most religious."* Religiousness for the Ancient Egyptians was total cosmic consciousness. The Egyptian concept is now commonly known in the East as *Sufism*, and in the West as *alchemy*.

This book explains how Ancient Egypt is the root of present-day Sufism/alchemy, and how the mystics of Egypt camouflage their practices under a thin layer of Islam. This book will also show how other peoples tried to adopt the Egyptian model, but fell short and ended up with partial and incomplete applications. The Egyptian mystical teachings and practices are markedly different from those practiced by Sufis in other countries, as is shown throughout this book.

The Egyptian model of mysticism is not about the outer world, or a community of believers, or dogma, scriptures, rules, or rituals. It is not simply believing that God is this, or God is that or that. It is not just asking one to "believe" and one is automatically in God's graces. The Egyptian model of mysticism consists of ideas and practices that provide the tools for any spiritual seeker to progress along each's alchemical Path towards "union with the Divine".

This spiritual Path towards union requires one to engage in the hard, and sometimes painful (but joyful), commitment to inner and outer purification. The spiritual seeker must gain knowledge of reality/truth, do well in everything, and apply what he/she has learned in the world. It is a philosophy of life, a way of individual behavior in order to achieve the highest morality and internal happiness and peace.

The general perception of mysticism is that it is possible to achieve communion with God, by attaining knowledge of spiritual truth through intuition acquired by fixed meditation. The Egyptian model for gaining knowledge is based on the utilization of both intellect and intuition.

In the Egyptian model, there are no "chosen people" who are picked by God or a religious authority. One must seek the Divine—through a hard labor of love. Those who succeed in achieving union with the Divine are chosen and venerated by the masses.

This book is intended to clarify these facts and to shed light on the Egyptian mystical model (Sufism)—yet not too much light, because that could endanger the traditions and their practitioners under the present ever-threatening dark cloud of Islam.

Moustafa Gadalla
To-beh 1, 13,001 (Ancient Egyptian Calendar)
January 9, 2003 CE

Standards and Terminology

1. You may find variations in writing the same Ancient Egyptian term, such as **Amen/Amon/Amun** or **Pir/Per**. This is because the vowels you see in translated Egyptian texts are only approximations of sounds, which are used by Egyptologists to help them pronounce the Ancient Egyptian terms/words.

2. The Ancient Egyptian word, **neter**, and its feminine form **netert**, have been wrongly, and possibly intentionally, translated to *god* and *goddess*, by almost all academicians.

   Neteru (plural of **neter/netert**) are the divine principles and functions of the One Supreme God.

3. When referring to the names of cities, Pharaohs, **neteru**, etc., if the commonly used Greek name is different than the true Egyptian name, we will show the correct Egyptian name **in this font**, followed by the "Westernized common" Greek rendering between parentheses.

4. The term *Baladi* will be used throughout this book to denote the present silent majority of Egyptians, who adhere to the Ancient Egyptian traditions, under a thin exterior layer of Islam.

The Christian population of Egypt is an ethnic minority that came as refugees, from Judaea and Syria to the Ptolemaic/Roman-ruled Alexandria. Now, 2,000 years later, they are still easily distinguishable in looks and mannerisms from the majority of native Egyptians. [See *Exiled Egyptians: The Heart of Africa*, by same author, and our website (http://www.egypt-tehuti.org), for detailed information.]

5.   The term *Islamized* instead of *Moslem/Muslim* will be used throughout the book. The term *Islamized* describes the actual conditions of people described as *Moslems*. The word *Moslem* is indicative of a person's free will to practice Islam. However, since Islam was forced on people many centuries ago, and because present-day born-Moslems are subject to execution by any Moslem (according to the Koran) if they renounce their religion, it is more appropriate to call these hapless people *Islamized* and not *Moslems*.

6.   Throughout this book, the fonting of quotations varies depending on the source of quotation. There are generally two types of fonting:

This font is used to refer to Ancient Egyptian sources.

This font is used to refer to quotes from other sources.

Chronology of Egyptian Dynasties

Neolithic Period	before 5000 BCE
Pre-dynastic Period	c. 5000-3300 BCE
Protodynastic Period	c. 3300-3050 BCE

Dynasty	Dates	
I	3050 BCE - 2890 BCE ⎤	Early
II	2890 BCE - 2649 BCE ⎬	Dynastic
III	2649 BCE - 2575 BCE ⎦	Period
IV	2575 BCE - 2465 BCE ⎤	Old
V	2465 BCE - 2323 BCE ⎬	Kingdom
VI	2323 BCE - 2150 BCE ⎦	
VII-X - 1st Interm. Per.	2150 BCE - 2040 BCE	
XI	2040 BCE - 1991 BCE ⎤	Middle
XII	1991 BCE - 1783 BCE ⎦	Kingdom
XIII-XVII - 2nd Inter. Per.	1783 BCE - 1550 BCE	
XVIII	1550 BCE - 1307 BCE ⎤	New
XIX	1307 BCE - 1196 BCE ⎬	Kingdom
XX	1196 BCE - 1070 BCE ⎦	
XXI	1070 BCE - 712 BCE ⎤	3rd
XXII	945 BCE - 712 BCE ⎬	Intermed.
XXIII	878 BCE - 712 BCE ⎬	Period
XXIV	740 BCE - 712 BCE ⎦	
XXV	712 BCE - 657 BCE ⎤	
XXVI	664 BCE - 525 BCE ⎬	
XXVII (Persian)	525 BCE - 404 BCE ⎬	Late
XXVIII	404 BCE - 399 BCE ⎬	Kingdom
XXIX	399 BCE - 380 BCE ⎬	
XXX	380 BCE - 343 BCE ⎦	
Second Persian Period	343 BCE - 332 BCE	
Macedonian Kings	332 BCE - 304 BCE ⎤	
Ptolemaic Dynasty	323 BCE - 30 BCE ⎬	Greco-Roman
Roman Emperors	30 BCE - 323 CE ⎬	Period
Byzantine Emperors	323 CE - 642 CE ⎦	

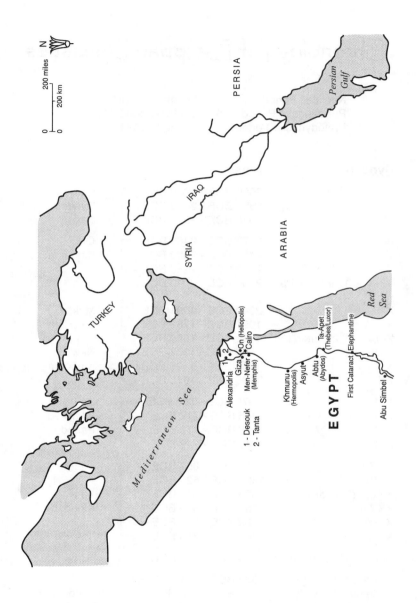

Map of Egypt and Surrounding Countries

Part
I
The Hidden Treasure

1

Egyptian Mysticism and Islamized Sufism

Dogmatic and Mystical Routes

Mankind is always trying to understand its own reason for existence, relative to the universe in which it finds itself placed. There are generally two routes in which to search for the answers:

1. **The dogmatic religions**, whose basic assumption is that of a personal God who rules the universe and who communicates his will to man through prophets and lawgivers. This God is directly and personally concerned with the right ordering of this world, and with the right and righteous relationships he wishes to exist between man and man. Hence, he is the ultimate lawgiver. Christianity, Judaism, and Islam fall under this category.

2. **The mystics**, who do not believe in a personal God, for to call him God at *all* can only mislead, for *He* is not a person, *It* is a principle—it is the principle of unchanging Being that is yet the source of all becoming, the stillness that is yet the source of all activity, the One from which all multiplicity proceeds. This book will explain the Egyptian model of mysticism.

Egyptians: The Most Religious

The Greek historian Herodotus (500 BCE) stated:

Of all the nations of the world, the Egyptians are the happiest, healthiest and most religious.

The excellent condition of the Egyptians was attributed to their application of metaphysical realities in their daily life, in other words—total cosmic consciousness. *As above so below and as below so above* was the main law of existence for them—there was no perceived difference between sacred and mundane. Every action, no matter how mundane, was in some sense a cosmic corresponding act: plowing, sowing, reaping, brewing, playing games—all were viewed as earthly symbols for divine activities. The scenes of daily activities, found inside Egyptian tombs, show a strong perpetual correlation between the earth and heavens.

In Egypt, what we now call religion was so widely acknowledged that it did not even need a name, because it is life itself in all its aspects. All their knowledge that was based on cosmic consciousness was embedded into their daily practices, which became traditions.

The mystical torch of the Ancient Egyptians has continued, through the practices and traditions of the silent majority—*Baladi* Egyptians. Some of the *Baladi* Egyptians dedicate themselves to further spiritual enlightenment. These mystics of Egypt are called *"Sufis"* by others. Just like their ancestors, present-day Egyptian mystics dislike being given any inclusive name that might force them into doctrinal conformity. The Egyptian mystical seekers prefer to call themselves *Seekers of Ways*. Egyptian mysticism, now known as *"Sufism"*, is (now) a name without reality. It once was a reality without a name. We only use the term *mystics* or *Sufis* here, to identify them to the readers.

A *Seeker of the Way* is anyone who believes that it is possible to have direct experience of God and who seeks such a Path. The Egyptian model of mysticism is a natural expression of personal religion in relation to the expression of religion as a communal matter. It is an assertion of a person's right to seek contact with the source of being and reality, as opposed to institutionalized religion, which is based on authority, a one-way Master-slave relationship, with its emphasis upon ritual observance and a legalistic morality.

The Source of Sufism

The common premise is that *"Sufism" is an Islamic group practicing a form of mysticism that originated in Persia.*

As the book progresses, we will find that *"Sufism"* has nothing to do with Islam or Persia, and everything to do with the quiet people of Ancient and *Baladi* Egypt. Two points of interest should be mentioned here:

1. The term and practices of *"Sufism"* surfaced as a result of Islamic conquests and the subsequent terrorizing of its victims. In order for the Islamic-terrorized masses to maintain their ancient traditions, they had to camouflage old traditions under an Islamic garment.

2. The pure form of *"Sufism"* originated in Egypt. Other countries copied it and were quick to take the credit for it. Their application of *"Sufism"* is impure and incomplete, as we will find throughout this book.

The common premise (mentioned above) about the roots and essence of *"Sufism"* is absolutely wrong, as we will conclude by examining the facts throughout this book. Here are just a few introductory facts:

1. The notion of an Islamic origin of *"Sufism"* is wrong. *"Islamic mysticism"* is an oxymoron—as per the following selected points:

- The mystical seekers who are called *"Sufis"* have always suffered from Islamic rule throughout the ages. Many have been killed. They have been accused of attempting to make innovations on the dogmas of Islam; of following practices forbidden by the Koran; of denying the very existence of a personal Allah. The tolerance, or lack thereof, of Sufism in the Arabized/Islamized world is closely linked to the whim of the ruler and how he interprets/enforces Islamic laws. During certain periods, Sufism was/is tolerated; during others, it was outlawed and condemned.

- The keynote of mysticism (Sufism) is the union between man and God, which in Islam is considered blasphemy; and as such punishable by death by any Moslem, as "empowered" by the Koran itself!

- Islamic teachings are characterized by a consuming fear of God's wrath, while the Egyptian model of mysticism (Sufism) emphasizes love and not fear. God is perceived in terms of emotional closeness—"the friend," "the lover"—whose love can be experienced personally and individually.

- Mysticism (Sufism) is based on self-attained revelations by mystical means, which is contrary to Islam. Such revelations, as experienced by the mystical seekers (Sufis), are considered blasphemy and therefore are punishable by death, as established in the Koran.

- The Egyptian mystical seekers (Sufis) include in

their ritual practices (as well as public festivals) specific methods to achieve ecstatic proximity to God—through music, dance, or song. This goes contrary to Islam—where music, singing, and dancing are strictly forbidden, as clearly stated in all treatises on Islamic laws.

- Contrary to Islamic doctrine, the Egyptian mysticism (Sufism) bridges the gulf between man and God with folk saints. Veneration of folk saints and pilgrimages to their shrines represent an important aspect of the Egyptian *Baladi* mystical practices, which is totally against the Islamic doctrine.

The above scene, from a stele dating about 4500 years ago, shows the Egyptian practices of veneration of folk saints, at their dome-roofed shrines, and presentations of offerings.

2. The claim of a Persian origin of *"Sufism"* is also wrong. The Persians themselves refer to Egypt as the source of *"Sufism"*. For example:

a. The Egyptian Dhu 'l-Nun (died in 860 CE) is recognized in all Islamized Sufi references as the spiritual source of *"Sufism"*, who prepared the way for the presently known form of Islamized Sufism. Sufis claim him for their own, as a leader and the originator of important concepts, such as the mystic's direct knowledge (gnosis) of God and the stations and states of the spiritual Path. Dhu 'l-Nun was knowledgeable of the Ancient Egyptian

hieroglyphs. A number of short treatises are attributed to him, which deal with alchemy, magic,
and medicine.

b. Tehuti (Thoth), the Ancient Egyptian **neter** (god), is recognized by
all early (and later) Sufi writers
as the ancient model of alchemy,
mysticism, and all related subjects.

The well known Sufi writer,
Idries Shah, admits the role of
Egypt via **Tehuti** and Dhu'I-Nun
on Sufism and alchemy as follows:

> . . . *alchemical lore came from Egypt direct from the
> writings of Tehuti (Thoth) . . . . According to Sufi tradition
> the lore was transmitted through Dhu'i-Nun the Egyp-
> tian, the King or Lord of the Fish, one of the most fa-
> mous of classical Sufi teachers. [The Sufis, 1964]*

Tehuti's name appears among the ancient masters
of what is now called the *Way of the Sufis*. In other
words, both the Sufis and the alchemists recognize **Tehuti** as the foundation of their knowledge.

Idries Shah also makes a direct reference to the
Spanish-Arab historian, Said of Toledo (died in
1069), who gives this tradition of the Ancient
Egyptian **Tehuti** (Thoth or Hermes):

> *Sages affirm that all antediluvian sciences originate with
> the Egyptian Hermes [Tehuti], in Upper Egypt* (namely
> Khmunu (Hermopolis)). *The Jews call him Enoch and
> the Moslems Idris. He was the first who spoke of the
> material of the superior world and of planetary move-
> ments . . . . Medicine and poetry were his functions . . .
> [as well as] the sciences, including alchemy and magic.*
> *[Cf. Asin Palacios, Ibn Masarra, p. 13]*

c. It is an indisputable fact that all Sufi mystical terms
are not Persian (or Turkish). All Sufi terms are
"Arabic". The "Arabic" language is substantially
of Egyptian origin. After the Arab/Islamic conquests of their neighboring countries (including
Egypt), they simply cancelled the identity of their
victimized countries, and labeled them "Arabs".

3. To continue the point above (regarding the language of
Sufism), it should be noted that the word, *Sufi*, was never
mentioned in the Koran or in Mohammed's sayings. There
is no consensus on its meaning. The "translation" of
the word/term *"Sufi"* as a *"wearer of wool"* is totally fab-
ricated, and is one of many attempted explanations.

The word is actually of Ancient Egyptian origin. **Seph/
Soph** was a component of common Egyptian names—
meaning *wisdom, purity* (among many other meanings).

4. Some of the standard Sufi terms that are often used are:
old religion, antique faith, old one, and *ancient tradition*.
Such terms were used/stressed by all early Sufi writers,
which is indicative of the pre-Islamic origins of Sufism.

5. The Egyptians are remarkably traditionalists to a fault.
Early historians have attested to this fact, such as:
Herodotus, in *The Histories, Book Two, 79*:

*The Egyptians keep to their native customs and never adopt
any from abroad.*

Herodotus, in *The Histories, Book Two, 91*:

*The Egyptians are unwilling to adopt Greek customs, or, to
speak generally, those of any other country.*

Plato and other writers affirmed the complete adherence of the Egyptians to their own traditions.

6. Supernatural powers acclaimed by the mystics (Sufis) are often called *magic*. From the earliest times, Egypt has been celebrated for its magicians, and accounts of their marvelous achievements have been documented— not only in Ancient Egyptian records, but also in the Bible and in the works of several of the classical writers. Furthermore, many of the tales in the famous collection of stories known as *The Arabian Nights* show what wonder-working powers were attributed to magicians in medieval Egypt.

Heka [shown herein] represents the Ancient Egyptian magical power of words. He is usually depicted holding two snakes with total ease.

7. The country that has the largest number of *"Sufi"* followers is Egypt. The participation in Sufi fellowships (orders) in other countries—besides Egypt—is very small by comparison.

Egyptian mysticism (Sufism) is not an offshoot of Islam; it is the old "religion" camouflaged into Arabized/Islamized terms. [See Appendix B—Sleeping With the Enemy (Surviving Islam)]

The Egyptian mystical seekers (Sufis) maintain low profiles, for they seek no public glory, but rather the ultimate mystical glory—The Divine.

2

The Treasure Within

The Image of God

Egyptian mysticism's (and likewise Sufism's) main keynote is the union— the identification of God and man.

It is commonly recognized by all theological and philosophical schools of thought that the human being is made in the image of God, i.e. a miniature universe; and that to understand the universe is to understand oneself, and vice versa.

Yet no culture has ever practiced the above principle like the Ancient Egyptians. Central to their complete understanding of the universe was the knowledge that man was made in the image of God, and as such, man represented the image of all creation. Accordingly, Egyptian symbolism has always related to man.

When we ask, "*Who is God?*" we are really asking, "*What is God?*". One can only define "God" through the multitude of "His" attributes / qualities / powers / actions. To know God is to know the numerous qualities of God. In other

words, the more we understand of the multiplicity of his actions, attributes, etc, the more we realize the totality of the
One—*The Unity of Multiplicity*. Far from being a primitive,
polytheistic form, this is the highest expression of monotheistic mysticism.

The concept of Egyptian monotheism can also apply to
man—the image of God. If we refer to, say, a person as Mr.
X, it means nothing to us. However, we begin to learn/know
more of Mr. X when we learn of his attributes, qualities,
actions, deeds, ...etc. A person who is an engineer, a father,
a husband, ... etc. does not have poly-personalities, but rather
a mono-personality with multiple functions/attributes. Man
is the perfect example of *Unity of Multiplicity*.

Within each human being is a "treasure," and this can
be found only by looking for it. The Egyptian model of mysticism unleashes the inner hidden potential of the human
being to learn, gain knowledge, and achieve.

Organs of Perception

Human faculties, although perceptive, are limited—like
a radio that can receive only certain electro-magnetic waves
and not other parts of the band. The perceived world is therefore a distortion. The inability to transcend the barrier of
our limited senses explains human shortcomings in understanding the complete reality of the world around us, in all
its aspects.

The flaw in Western culture is the inflation of the intellect at the expense of intuitive knowledge. This is one-di-
mensional mode of thought, which distorts the understanding of reality because it blocks other modes of consciousness.

The Egyptian mystics distinguish between the ordinary knowing of fact and the inner knowing of reality. Their activities connect and balance all these factors—understanding, being, and knowing. The Egyptian mystical goal is to establish equilibrium between the intellect and the inner faculties so that instead of canceling each other, they interact and enrich one another. Therefore, the Egyptian mystics develop their intuitive modes of consciousness to counterbalance the rational mode. The goal is to achieve equilibrium between the rational and non-rational modes of consciousness.

The main Egyptian mystical (Sufi) theme is the importance of consciousness, in integrating the inner faculties into comprehension through a gradual process. The Egyptian mystics refer to this process as using all organs of perception for a more comprehensive understanding.

Uniting/balancing and integrating complimentary opposites is one of the main and constant themes in Ancient Egypt. [More about this process in chapter 6.]

The Power of Love

For a person to excel in anything, one must love what one is doing. Love conquers all. Love makes everything easy. For the sake of reaching a goal, the lover feels no pain, struggle, obstacles, sacrifice, etc. towards their goal. Sufis call themselves *truth seekers*, *truth lovers*, which is reminiscent of the Ancient Egyptian **Ma-at** (representing the truth) *lovers* and *seekers* that permeate Ancient Egyptian texts. [More about **Ma-at** on page 45.]

The Egyptian mystical seeker is a philosopher, in the original meaning of the term (*philo* = love, *sophy* = truth).

To love the truth is to love the whole truth and nothing but the truth—no matter what the consequences are.

But love to the Egyptian mystical seeker (Sufi) means action, not merely enjoyment or even the despair of one-sided love. Love is the most powerful motivation, and must be both active and passive. Active love leads to seeking, action, determination, endurance, etc. The passive form of love is total surrender in order to receive, learn and absorb.

Man's love towards the Divine is a quality that manifests itself in the heart of the Divine seeker, in the form of veneration and magnification, so that he seeks to satisfy his Beloved and becomes impatient and restless in his desire for visions of Him, and cannot rest with anyone except Him. Love means attraction and being drawn to your Beloved—as powerful as a magnet. This powerful emotion/motivation is described as being crazy for/about the Beloved. Love is adoration, devotion, affection, passion, endearment and yearning. The yearning aspect of love is one of the most motivating forces in the whole journey of the return to the Divine Origin.

The goal of the Egyptian mystical seeker is to remove all the veils between himself/herself and God. The final veil is the "I"—the sense of separateness that we each carry. The philosophers (truth lovers) seek a similar path of love towards the Divine. For them, the goal is for the beloved, lover, and love to reunite—to become One.

With the power of love, the mystical aspirant can seek the Divine—through self-transformation.

Part
II
Transformation from Dust to Gold

3

The Alchemist Way

Atum/Adam: The Alchemist Goal

In Judaism, Christianity, and Islam, Adam is considered to be the first human being. In Sufi traditions, Adam symbolizes the *"Perfect Person (Man)"*.

The above-mentioned common beliefs are of Ancient Egyptian origin, as follows:

Atum/Atam/Adam

1. When the name, *Adam*, is written in the equivalent Ancient Egyptian alphabetical characters, it becomes **Atam/Atum.** In the Ancient Egyptian traditions, **Atam/Atum** represents the first realization of existence, and as such, he is depicted in full human form.

2. **Atam/Atum** means *he who completes or perfects*. In other words, **Atam** represents the Perfect Person. **Atam/Atum,** in the *Litany of Ra*, is recognized as the *ALL*.

In the *Unas Funerary* (so-called *Pyramid*) *Texts*, there is the following invocation:
   Salutation to thee, Atam,
   . . . .
   Thou art high in this thy name High Mound, ... [§1587]

The high mound where **Adam/Atam/Atum** stands is the Ancient Egyptian **Ben** stone, known in Sufi traditions as the *Philosopher's Stone* or the *Alchemist Stone*—the agent believed to transmute baser metals into gold and to prolong life indefinitely. This alchemist/Sufi tradition—of transforming matter (**Ben**) into gold (**Neb**), is of an Ancient Egyptian origin, as reflected in their language as follows:

- **Ben** has several related meanings: the *primordial stone*, the *mound of creation*, the *first state of matter*, *opposition/ negation*, *it is not, there is not, multiplicity*.
- The mirror image of **Ben** is **Neb** (**Ben** spelled backwards), which also has several related meanings: *gold* (traditionally the finished perfected end product—the goal of the alchemist), *lord, master, all, affirmation, pure*.

This **Ben** and **Neb** mirror image mode/theme permeated Ancient Egyptian thinking, and was later adopted into the Islamized Sufi traditions in the following ideas:

- the metaphor of the mirror
- reality and image (God and Man)
- the metaphor of the broken pieces
- the concept of duality
- reversing the Path from/to God is a mirror image (**Ben** to **Neb**).   [See chapter 6 for more details about all above points.]

The transformation from **Ben** (matter) to **Neb** (gold) is analogous to the alchemist traditions, which draw a parallel between metal and spiritual purification.

The Ancient Egyptian alchemical knowledge was, according to Sufi traditions, transmitted through Dhu'i-Nun the Egyptian (died in 860 CE), from the *Thrice-Great* **Tehuti** (Thoth) as the reputed originator of alchemy, by all Islamized Sufi sources. His name appears among the ancient masters of what is now called the *Way of the Sufis*.

Progressive Sowing and Reaping

The progress of the spiritual life is described as a journey or a pilgrimage consisting of slow progressions toward the goal of union with Reality. The Path/Way is a practical method to guide a mystical seeker through a succession of "stages", toward the ultimate goal of unification with the Divine. The "stages" of the journey have been variously described in the Islamized Sufi traditions as consisting of 7, 10, etc. stages. Such progressive stages are clearly described in the countless Ancient Egyptian transformational (funerary) texts—detailing the journey of the successful soul from its earthly living—towards the Divine.

Each "stage" of the Path is acquired through striving, and is a matter of conscious disciplined action. Whenever an aspirant achieves a certain level of personal development, he is rewarded psychologically with certain spiritual liberation. As such, the Path/Way consists of spiritual stations and corresponding spiritual states. Stages are steps taken by us—rising/ascending. The "states" form a similar psychological chain. The experiences of the spiritual states feel like liberations/releases that descend into one's heart. That sense of relief is equivalent to untying the knots—a problem/question has been resolved. Such experience will elevate the mystical seeker to a higher level, where he/she can continue to learn, using both intellect and intuition.

Your Guiding Angels

In order for the Egyptian mystical seeker to attain his goal and reach the end of his journey, he is advised to follow the directions of a leader who lays down for him certain rules of practice, and guides him in every detail of his life. It is much easier to have a spiritual guide in the earlier stages of the spiritual development, because there is a human tendency to overlook our own obstacles—to ignore them or deny their existence even when we have seen them clearly. Therefore, it is difficult for us to achieve and sustain spiritual clarity without someone other than ourselves leading us beyond our own shortcomings. As such, it is understood that at some point in your development you will need to work with a guide/coach, which is known in strict Islamized countries as *sheikh* (the same term for Islamic clergy).

The guide assists the mystical aspirants in moving closer to realizing their inner nature. By helping us to reconnect with our own inner wisdom, the guide empowers and enables us to continue the pilgrimage back to ourselves.

The guide teaches out of his or her own personal understanding and fullness of being. The guide is someone who has successfully passed the first two stages of purification and attainment of knowledge [see page 37]. The guide's role consists of a combination of a guide/ coach/ teacher/ soulmate/ friend/ pilot/ navigator/ spiritual medium. There are a variety of guides with different capabilities. In larger mystic (Sufi) fellowships (orders), there are usually several guides who work as a "coaching" team to guide the mystical aspirant through his spiritual progression. The most prominent functions of the guide are:

1. **As a guide**, he shows the way—but the aspirant must himself do the walking. Man must develop by his own effort toward growth of an evolutionary nature, stabilizing his consciousness. The guide leads his disciple from the beginning of his journey to its end, guiding him at every 'stage' and helping him in every 'state'.

2. **As a friend**, he is a companion and advisor, who provides reassurance, and a point of view that is influenced by his perception of the other's need.

3. **As a soulmate**, he establishes a relationship and means of communication between himself and the mystical seeker that transcends the conventional relationship between a teacher and a learner, since a part of the teaching and learning stands outside time and space. The process of learning depends on the degree of reciprocity of the candidate, through his experience with the teacher and not on an argumentative basis. The guide, as such, is more than just one who passes on formal knowledge. As such, the relationship between them is formed as an affectionate bond, in which spiritual support and protection are maintained.

4. **As a spiritual medium,** he connects (through the spiritual lineage of a fellowship) with the founder of the mystic fellowship—**Pir/Mir/ Wali**. This founder is the person who, while alive on earth, has achieved all three levels of consciousness [see page 37], and thus became/ becomes a permanent power in the higher realms.
In other words, the **Pir/Mir/Wali** is the completed human being from whom the particular mystical (Sufi) fellowship derives its **Ba-ra-ka** (spiritual powers). The guide, through his spiritual training and attainment, is able to 'transmit' spiritual power from the founder-**Pir** to his mystical aspirants.

It should be noted that both the mystical seekers and their guides have their own incomes and their relationship is void of any financial exchange.

[More about the role of the guide and the spiritual chain/lineage throughout the book, especially chapter 11 and Appendix C.]

The Thrice Tehuti

In Ancient Egyptian traditions, the *words* of **Ra** (Re), revealed through **Tehuti** (equivalent to *Hermes* or *Mercury*), became the things and creatures of this world, i.e. the words (meaning sound energies) created the forms in the universe. As such, **Tehuti** (Thoth) represents the link between the meta-physical (extrahuman) and the physical (terrestrial).

Early Islamized Sufi traditions describe **Tehuti** (Thoth) of Egypt as the **neter** (god) who:

- was the link between the extra-human and the terrestrial.

- like the aspiring mystic, **Tehuti** is represented as a bird. Sometimes he is a man with the head of an ibis, where the head would indicate aspiration or attainment in the mind, localized in the head.

- moved, like Mercury (his equivalent), at immense speed, negating time and space, in the same way that inner experience does.

- is an athlete, a developed man.

- is shown as a matured man, a man of age and wisdom. As such, **Tehuti** is associated with a form of wisdom that is transmitted to man from divine sources.

- created the lyre with three strings, and through its music aroused in the hearers three levels of consciousness. **Tehuti's** music is the means of transmission and intermediation between human and divine. [More about this item throughout the book under the name, Samaa.]

Tehuti (Thoth) is commonly known as *Thrice Tehuti*, representing the three levels of consciousness. A new/raised consciousness is equivalent to a new awakening. In Sufi traditions, each of the three levels of consciousness are referred to as *death—rebirth*. The same thinking has pervaded Ancient (and present-day) Egypt, where *birth and rebirth* is a constant theme. The word *death* is employed in a figurative sense. The theme that man must *"die before he dies"* or that he must be *"born again"* in his present life is taken symbolically, or is commemorated by a ritual. In this, the candidate has to pass through certain specific experiences (technically termed *"deaths"*). A good example is baptism, which was the main objective at Easter, after Lent—representing death of the old self by immersing into water, and the rising of the new/renewed self by coming out of the water.

The three levels of consciousness in the Egyptian mystical traditions are:

1. The purification process of body and soul. [See chapter 4.]

2. Gaining knowledge through both intellect and intuition (revelation). The objective, in simple terms, is to put the pieces of the cosmic puzzle together, but the lines separating the pieces are still visible. [See chapter 6.]

3. Vanishment into the Divine Essence through the cessation of all conscious thought. In the puzzle metaphor, it is when the puzzle is complete, and the mystic no longer sees the lines between the pieces. [See chapter 6.]

The mystical seeker must succeed in each of the these levels before advancing to the next higher level.

4

The Purification Process

Pure Gold (Purifying the Heart and Tongue)

The Ancient Egyptian transformational (funerary) texts are permeated with purity as a prerequisite for advancing to higher realms/heavens. The Egyptian model of mysticism stresses that purity can only be achieved through purifying the heart and practicing the pure intent in the ordinary daily life.

In the Ancient Egyptian traditions, the active faculties of **Atum/Atam/Adam** (The Perfect Man) were *intelligence*, which was identified with the heart and personified as **Heru** (Horus)—a solar **neter** (god), and *action*, which was identified with the tongue and personified as **Tehuti** (Thoth)—a lunar **neter**. The solar and lunar **neteru** stress his universal character. In the Shabaka Stele (dated from the 8th century BCE, but is a reproduction of a 3rd Dynasty text), we read:

> **There came into being as the heart (Heru), and there came into being as the tongue (Tehuti), the form of Atum.**

One thinks with the heart, and acts with the tongue, as described on the Shabaka Stele:

> **The Heart thinks all that it wishes, and the Tongue delivers all that it wishes.**

The significance of heart and tongue permeates Ancient Egyptian texts, and was subsequently adopted in *"Sufism"*.

Tehuti   Heru

The Ancient Egyptian depiction [shown herein] shows the Perfected Person being purified by the combined action of his heart (**Heru**) and tongue (**Tehuti**), with water in the form of the **ankh** and the **was**, which represents the lustral water. The **ankh** represents eternal life, and the **was** represents authority, i.e. total self-control.

Likewise, the aspirant, in the Egyptian model, learns to purify his inner-self by taming vices and practicing the opposites of such vices in society. Knowledge is gained by both the mind and that acquired by experience. The inner purification must be completed by practicing good social behavior in the ordinary daily life. Every action impresses itself upon the heart. The inward being of a person is really the reflection of his deeds and actions. Doing good deeds thus establishes good inner qualities; the virtues impressed upon the heart in turn govern the actions of the limbs. As each act, thought, and deed makes an image on the heart, it becomes an attribute of the person. This maturation of the soul through acquired attributes leads to progressive mystical visions and the ultimate unification with the Divine.

Reciprocally, the knowledge obtained by both intellect and intuition [discussed in chapter 6] is the source of virtue that must be practiced in ordinary life. The struggle for virtue and the vision of the Divine, are all aspects of a single progressive achievement in the course of which the aspirant becomes more wise, until he achieves the totality of being that entails mystical vision and ordinary piety simultaneously.

The Healthy Body

In our present times, we say, *"Cleanliness is next to Godliness,"* and *"Your body is a temple."* These premises have always been the view of the mystical Egyptians.

To have a healthy mind and spirit, one must have a healthy body and surroundings. In their conceptions of moral purity, the Ancient Egyptians always emphasized sanitary observances of the human body and surroundings.

The most sacred of Ancient Egyptian texts, such as the *Book of Coming Forth by Light* (commonly known as the *Book of the Dead*), emphasize:

• Maintaining a clean body, such as: frequent bathing, mouth washing, clipping and cleaning fingernails and toenails, shaving (including body hair), washing hands and feet, etc.

• Purity of the food. Herodotus (500 BCE) describes the measures taken by the Egyptians to ensure the ceremonial purity of sacrificial animals.

The ancient traditions emphasize maintaining good eating habits, with an attitude of *eat to live*—not *live to eat*. They also recommend going through cyclical internal cleansing by fasting (abstention from eating fish, meat, and dairy products for a cycle of 40 days), and other means.

Exercises and staying in shape were/are essential for the Ancient and the mystical *Baladi* Egyptians. The Ancient Egyptian King was not supposed (or even able) to reign unless he was in good health and spirit. The Pharaoh was required to run a 5-mile (8 km) course in the annual **Heb-Sed** rituals. [More about the healthy body in chapter 5, Basic Practices.]

A healthy and clean body is a prerequisite to all daily activities, in the Egyptian model of mystical seeking.

Getting Out of the Box

It is commonly understood that the figure of a cubical box represents the restraint of human potential.

The Egyptian was highly conscious of the box-like structure, which is the model of the earth or the material world. The form of statuary, called the *"cube statue"*, is prevalent since the Middle Kingdom (2040-1783 BCE). The subject was integrated into the cubic form of the stone. In these cube statues, there is a powerful sense of the subject emerging from the confinement of the cube. Its symbolic significance is that the spiritual principle is emerging from the material world. The earthly person is placed unmistakably in material existence.

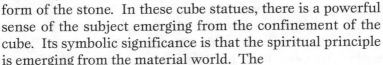

Cultivation of the desired virtues has the effect of liberating the aspirant from the material world by emerging from the box—the lower self.

The Divine person is shown sitting squarely on a cube i.e. mind over matter.

Other traditions, such as the *Platonic* and *Pythagorean*, adopted the same concept of the Egyptian cubic representation of the material world.

Battling the Enemies (Impurities) Within

There are basically two forces within each of us: one pulling us down into the box, and the other pulling us out of the box. This archetypal inner struggle in the Egyptian model is symbolized in the struggle between **Heru** (Horus) and **Set** (Seth). It is the archetypal struggle be-

Heru   Set

tween opposing forces. **Heru**, in this context, is the divine man, born of nature, who must do battle against **Set**, his own kin, representing the power of opposition and not *evil* in the narrow sense. **Set** represents the concept of opposition in all aspects of life (physically and metaphysically).

We must continuously learn and evolve, like **Heru** (Horus)—whose name means *He Who is Above*. In other words, we must strive to reach higher and higher. We learn and act by affirmation of the **Heru** in each of us, and by negating the **Set** within us. The obstacles within each of us, represented by **Set**, must be controlled and/or overcome.

In Ancient Egyptian temples, tombs, and texts, human vices are depicted as foreigners (the sick body is sick because it is/was invaded by foreign germs). Foreigners are depicted as subdued—arms tightened/tied behind their backs—to portray inner self-control. The most vivid example of self control is the common depiction of the Pharaoh (*The Perfected Man*), on the outer walls of Ancient Egyptian temples, subduing/controlling foreign enemies— the enemies (impurities) within.

To battle the enemies within, we must identify and acknowledge each of them. Stories and other means of expression [see Appendix D] personify bad manners such as arrogance, anger, envy, etc. The characters in the Egyptian stories will help you see these impurities in yourself (mirror image) so you can hate, reject, and defeat them. Other forms of expression such as proverbs and humor serve the same purpose.

We need to identify and control/cleanse the impurities within ourselves, which impede our judgment and ultimate objective.

The Ego – Personal Enemy #1

The supreme obstacle for the human being is his own egotistic consciousness that is dominated by pride, egotism, and self-centered greed and lust.

Controlling the ego was/is one of the most important ethical requirements in the Egyptian model of mysticism. One of the Egyptian King's titles was, *The Most Humble*. His abode while on earth was made of mud-brick—the same material used by the humblest peasants.

To cultivate humility, the mystical aspirant must consider himself a servant. The aspirants practice humility by serving others without exception. The richest and most educated of the Egyptian mystics (Sufis) are found begging on street corners, serving water to the public, cleaning bathrooms, etc.

The Ancient Egyptian transformational (funerary) texts show that one must overcome many obstacles on one's way towards the ultimate reunification. The main obstacle is the ego. To reunite with the Divine, we must be ego-free.

The symbolic Ancient Egyptian scene [shown above] depicts **Heru** (Horus) and his four disciples (sons), each armed with a knife, demonstrating to **Ausar** (Osiris) their success in controlling the ego. Their success is symbolized by the ass-headed man (symbol of the ego in man), with knives stuck in his body and bound by his arms to the forked stick.

In an Ancient Egyptian Instruction given in 2380 BCE to a soon-to-be high official, the words begin as follows:

Do not be arrogant because you are learned; do not be over-confident because you are well informed. Consult the ignorant man as well as the wise one.

There is a significant difference between the Egyptian mystical (Sufi) model and that of the Asian versions of Sufism—in particular the Persian version. While humility is the paramount feature of Egyptian teachings, other versions are the exact opposite. While Egyptians don't associate their extensive wisdom texts to individuals, the Persians love to brag—describing their "writers" as "incomparable", "incredible", "inimitable" in the titles of their "booklets", such as:

The Exploits of the Incomparable Mulla Nasrudin
The Pleasantries of the Incredible Mulla Nasrudin
The Subtleties of the Inimitable Mulla Nasrudin

It should come as no surprise that these and other similar "un-humble" titles are totally void of wisdom, for humility is a prerequisite to wisdom.

The Do's and Don'ts

To achieve inner purification, one must cultivate good manners (affirmation) and suppress bodily impulses (negations). Inner purification can only be achieved through both learning and practicing [as explained on page 39].

The Ancient Egyptian wisdom has always laid great emphasis on the cultivation of ethical behavior and service to society. The constant theme of the Egyptian wisdom literature was the 'acting out' of Truth—**Maa-Kheru**—on earth.

Ma-at [shown herein] represents the truth, the Way. She is always depicted wearing the feather of truth on her head. Likewise, the Sufis speak of the Path/Way and seeking the truth.

In Ancient Egypt, the concept of **Ma-at** has permeated all Egyptian writings, from the earliest times and throughout Egyptian history. **Ma-at**, *The Way*, encompasses the virtues, goals, and duties that define the acceptable, if not ideal, social interaction and personal behavior. **Ma-at** is maintained in the world by the correct actions and personal piety of its adherents.

A summary of the Egyptian conception of righteousness can be found in what is popularly known as the *Negative Confessions*. A more detailed picture of a righteous man and the expected conduct and the ideas of responsibility and retribution can be obtained from the walls of tomb-chapels and in several literary compositions that are usually termed as wisdom texts. Among them are the 30 chapters of *The Teaching of Amenemope*, which contain collections of poetic phrases of moral content and advice. Such teaching was later copied in the Old Testament's *Book of Proverbs*.

In addition to the different modes of learning [as referred

to in Appendix D], there were additional practical wisdom texts of systematic instructions, composed of maxims and precepts. [See *Egyptian Cosmology: The Animated Universe* by same author for samples.]

To be liberated from one's box, the mystical aspirant must look himself/herself in the mirror, so to speak—and must both negate (refrain) vices and affirm (cultivate) virtues. For example:

1. Refrain from such vices as: envy, backbiting, and purge ignorance, uncharitableness, the ego, laziness, over-confidence, arrogance, evasiveness, indifference, gluttony, vices of speech, anger, hypocrisy, conceit, etc.

2. Cultivate virtues such as:
- Recognition of a fault and ensuring that it will never happen again. (repentance)
- Fortitude and gratitude.
- Single-hearted devotion, love, yearning/longing.
- Resolve, truthfulness.
- Contemplation, self-examination, and self-evaluation.
- Patience.
- Silence and listening.
- Hunger for knowledge.
- Humility.
- Satisfaction/contentment.
- Servanthood.
- Willpower/determination.
- Righteousness by following the straight path.
- Sincerity.

We must continuously critique ourselves. We must continue to contemplate, evaluate, act, re-examine, ...over and over again.

The Pauper is a Prince

To be liberated from the box, the aspirant must reject the confinement of the material world. Material wealth must not be the goal of the mystical aspirant. In the Egyptian model, the mystical aspirant must work, but not be enslaved in compiling wealth. Being wealthy is fine, as long as becoming wealthy is not the main objective. The Egyptian mystic ideal of materialistic poverty is a lack of desire for wealth. The ascending reward for material apathy is the feeling of contentment and peace of mind. It is a sort of liberation from the box—the material world.

One must be full of bountifulness and generosity, i.e. give back of yourself, time, money, etc. Material apathy means living a simple, moderate life—not to extremes.

In the unique Egyptian mystical model, humility of spirit and demeanor are required from all; they are taught not to consider themselves superior to others, but to rank themselves as the poorest, lowest, and most humble of mankind. It is therefore that these mystics are distinguished by the deep humility of their manner. Their heads are ever bent, their gaze absorbed. As a result, they have tolerance and goodwill to all mankind, irrespective of race or creed.

Once the person is pure (body, mind, and spirit), the aspirant has succeeded in reaching the first level of consciousness.

The second level is gaining knowledge through both intellect and spiritual experience (revelation). At this time, the aspirant must join (if he did not join earlier) a mystic fellowship—compatible with his personality—in order to find a spiritual guide and to participate in group activities.

5

Basic Practices

The first stage of purification [chapter 4] is vastly improved by performing/following special practices. These practices become essential for advancement in the second and third (final) stages of the Spiritual Path [details in chapter 6].

The Power of Concentration

Concentration is necessary for serious contemplation (thoughtful inspection/study). It is the only way to put things together. The more (and deeper) the aspirant concentrates, the more expansive his horizon becomes. Therefore, exercises to improve concentration are essential for the mystical seeker. Some basic exercises used by the mystical seekers include: playing games, juggling, sports, board games, musical training, whirling, etc.

One of the most profound (yet simple) practices is to train the eyes not to be distracted by the phenomenal world. This is accomplished by blindfolding the eyes for gradually longer periods of time. As a result, the mystical seekers learn not to be distracted by superficialities in the phenomenal world.

Concentration skills are also beneficial in all other practices/activities, such as breathing, playing music, etc.

Advanced concentration practices must be performed under strict supervision by qualified guides. Such practices without supervision are harmful and possibly dangerous.

The Animated Breathing Techniques

The term *breath* has special significance to the Egyptian mystic, because it resonates on both the physical and spiritual levels. The breath of life is known in Ancient Egypt as **Amen/Amon/Amun**. He represents the hidden or occult force underlying creation. The Ancient Egyptian papyrus known as the *Leiden Papyrus* describes **Amen** as:

> He [who] gives birth to everything that is and causes all that exists to live.

In the Egyptian mystical traditions, learning breathing rhythms is essential in the ecstatic practice known as *zikr*, which involves controlled breathing rhythms, dancing, and the chanting of musical compositions.

The Egyptian mystic learns to breathe music. The natural breathing rhythm is reflected in the binary and ternary method of time measurement in musical performance. When a person is in a quiet sleep, the time between expiration and inhalation is twice as long as that between inhalation and exhalation. The underlying binary or ternary rhythm is known as the *fundamental rhythm*. Subdivisions of these beats that appear within the general musical framework are called the *subsidiary rhythm*.

Breathing practices must be taught and supervised by qualified mystical guides.

Playing the Magic Flute (and other instruments)

Concentration and breathing techniques are taught and practiced by Egyptian mystics (Sufis), while learning to play musical instruments—

especially wind instruments such as the end-blown reed pipe (*nay*) and *mizmar* (double clarinets). The Egyptian *nay* player led, and continues to lead, all religious processions in both Ancient and present-day festivals.

The end-blown reed pipe (*nay*) is most often used to sharpen the skills of the mystical seeker, because it perfects coordination, breathing, concentration, rhythm, etc. Its playing requires a lot of patience. The player requires a considerable finesse. In order to achieve any desired tone, the player must control, coordinate, and manipulate: the strength and direction of his breath; the tension of his lips; the movement of his tongue; the position of the lip and head; as well as opening or closing the fingerholes in diverse combinations.

Since a single *nay* (end-blown flute) with a certain length can only provide a limited number of musical pitches, the Egyptian musicians (then and now) used/use a set of seven different lengths of *nays*, in order to change the tonality, and/or to change the pitch. Their lengths range from 26.8" (68cm) to 14.8" (37.5cm).

Playing other musical instruments are also important, such as double reed-pipes, *tri-kanun* (zithers), short-necked lutes (*oud*), *kamangas* (violins), horns, clappers, cymbals, castanets, small drums, and tambourines. Music plays an important role in the ancient and present-day practices and festivals. [More about the role of music in chapter 10 and Appendix C.]

Recitations of Names, Rosaries, etc.

To achieve higher concentration, Egyptian mystics guide their disciples through a graduated series of different forms of ejaculatory prayers, performed for daily recitation chiefly with the help of a rosary. Egyptian beads were always an important part of their rituals, for over 5000 years.

Recitations consist of repeating a word, name, or a phrase numerous times. This is reminiscent of the Ancient Egyptians' *Litany of Ra (Re)*—The Creator. The Litany begins with a brief preface, then is followed by 75 invocations to the names/forms of Ra, followed by a series of prayers and hymns. Each recited name represents a specific aspect/attribute of Ra.

The Ancient Egyptian texts provide an extensive number and variety of litanies, rosaries, eulogies, psalms, hymns, etc. Likewise, present-day Egyptian mystics (Sufis) utilize the same ancient poetic and recitative compositions.

Egyptian mystics have a countless number of these poetic and musical compositions that they know by heart. Each composition is sung/recited at a specific time and on specific occasions. These hundreds of Egyptian compositions are too old to be accredited to specific authors.

Recitation of names and rosaries are important in the ecstatic practice of *zikr*. The mystical rosaries (*awrad*) are usually a long well-composed series, in the form of poetic stanzas of recitations. Each rosary consists of well designed components/sections, with each's own particular climaxes. These rosaries are replete with wise proverbial sayings, pious reflections, and moral precepts. The leader of the *zikr* chooses (and frequently modifies) the rosaries required for each practice—to fit the event, the level of participants, ...etc.
[See pages 62-3 and Appendix C for details about the *zikr*].

Sports and Rhythmic Movements

Maintaining a healthy athletic body was/is essential in the Egyptian model. Such perfect conditioning is attributed to the Patron of Alchemy—**Tehuti** (Thoth). Diodorus, in *Book I* (16), wrote:

> *It was by Tehuti (Hermes), for instance, according to the Egyptians, that . . . . he was the first . . . .* **to establish a wrestling school, and to give thought to the rhythmical movement of the human body and its proper development.** *. . . .*

Wrestling [as shown below, from an Ancient Egyptian tomb] is one of the many sports that is practiced by present-day mystical seekers (Sufis).

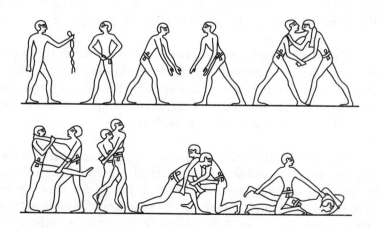

Rhythmic movements/exercises/games that are practiced by the mystical seekers include, but are not limited to: yoga, martial arts, wrestling, etc. A unique Egyptian rhythmic

ritual/game is the per-
forming of routines with
wooden swords [as shown
herein]. This is a very ritualistic and graceful game
that requires immense
concentration and talent.

The benefits of sports are very important in the life of
the mystic, since it combines the benefit of concentration,
proper breathing, and above all maintaining a healthy body
to maintain a healthy mind.

Other sports that are practiced by the
Egyptian mystics include: horsemanship,
running, etc. The Pharaoh, as the Perfected Man, was required to maintain perfect physical condition and he was required to go through annual endurance exercises such as running.

Mind Games

People of all
classes and the **neteru**
(gods/goddesses)
themselves are de-
picted playing all
types of games in An-
cient Egyptian tombs
and temples. Such
games included board

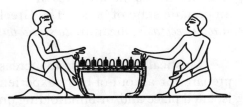

Game of drafts. Beni Hassan
and **Ta-Apet** (Thebes).

games, as well as physical activities and sporting events.

Ancient and classical writers affirmed that games owe their development, if not their very origin, to religious observances. Many accounts of games are mentioned by Homer as essential to the accompaniment of devotional ceremonies.

Games sharpen concentration, memory, patterns, etc, and in the process participants are having fun.

Contemplating Death (Astral Travel)

The interest shown by the Egyptians in their fate after death arose in part from their passionate interest in life itself. This is confirmed by people with near death experiences who come back with a zest for life and a sense of goodness and service. This is summed up by Montaigne, who said,

"He who would teach men to die, would teach them to live".

In order for the Egyptian mystical seeker to learn about the world of existence that lies beyond the limitations of our human senses, he must be able to free his soul from his body. In other words, he must reach an ecstatic state of being. The Greek origin of the word *ecstacy* is *ecstasis*, meaning *to stand outside oneself.*

Mystical seekers learn to increase their focus in order to prepare for an out-of-body experience, by entering a dark, isolated place and/or blindfolding one's eyes. Some mystical seekers lay down in a makeshift coffin and imagine that his/her soul hovers over his/her body.

Later training allows this part of you to travel to adjoining rooms, etc.

Group Astral Travel Practices

In order to gain knowledge (gnosis) through ecstatic revelations, members of the Egyptian mystic fellowships (Orders) perform a group practice, commonly known as *zikr*. This practice achieves the connectedness of body, mind, and spirit, which the Egyptian mystical seekers use to induce the ecstacy that leads to gaining knowledge of the world, which lies beyond the limitations of our human senses.

The practice consists of using breath control, head and body movements, and chanting in a ritualistic dance, performed to tunes provided by musicians and singers.

[More about the *zikr* in next chapter and in Appendix C.]

Enduring Love (Mind Over Matter)

The sensation of spiritual liberation comes as a result of the triumph of mind over matter. The gradual training of the mind makes it overcome/tolerate pain. This pain threshold is progressively expanded by gradational training. Ultimately, one feels no pain. Endurance is important to achieve any goal in life, as per the common saying: *"No pain, no gain."*

The Egyptian mystical fellowship of *Rifaiya* is remarkable for the wonderful way in which their spiritual exaltation triumphs over pain and physical limitations. Their walking in fire and eating the white hot embers, also glass and poisonous creatures—things which normally cause death or the most grievous bodily disturbances—have never been explained on material grounds. They usually show their talents in Egyptian *mouleds*, especially in the *El Desouki Mouled* [see page 95 for additional information].

6

The Way to Revelations

No Chosen People

In the Egyptian model of mysticism, revelations are accessible to anyone who aspires to seek them. There are no "special" people chosen by God to receive His revelations. In the hierarchy of existence, the human being is the image of the First Principle. By using his capacity for knowledge, the human being may ascend to the highest levels by contemplating his own reality in the mirror of God's existence.

Egyptian mysticism encompasses basically two types of spiritual experience.

1. A quest for spiritual self-development in the form of ethical self-control and worldly personal religious insight. The aspirant who is able to purify himself [see chapter 4] is ready now for the second quest.

2. The quest to find God in the manifested world as well as finding the manifested world in God. This is accomplished through gaining knowledge by using both intellect and intuition in order to transcend the limitations of our human senses. [Developing intuitive modes of consciousness will be explained later in this chapter and is detailed in Appendix C.]

Ra—The Unity of Multiplicity

The ultimate goal of the Egyptian mystical seekers is to realize Unity in multiplicity and multiplicity in the Unity of the universe. In Ancient Egyptian traditions, **Ra** (Re) represents the primeval, cosmic, creative force. **The Litany** describes **Ra** as **The One Joined Together, Who Comes Out of His Own Members**. The Ancient Egyptian definition of **Ra** is:

1. the perfect representation of the Unity that comprises the putting together of the many diverse entities.

2. **Ra's** twin term (**The One Joined Together, Who Comes Out of His Own Members**) shows the two-step metaphor of the puzzle [see page 37]—step one of joining the pieces, and step two of seeing all the pieces as one unit.

Ra (Re) is written as a circle with a dot or point in the center. The symbol for **Ra** represents both ends of the alchemical spiritual path, as follows:

- Center   = cause/nothingness
- Circumference = effect/manifestation

The mirror image of both ends of the Path (**Ben** and **Neb**) is used in the metaphor of the *reflective mirror*, in order to understand the universe and its cosmic unity. The mirror is the means to reconcile opposites and to perceive the connection between 'the phenomenal world' and the 'spiritual world' and thus understanding the 'multiplicity in unity'.

At earlier stages, man sees only pieces of things because his mind is fixed in a pattern designed to see things piece-meal, controlled by the limitation of a few senses. By healing the multiplicity within, the mystic experiences the world as whole and unified. There is only one Essence and all manifestations of that One Essence are in reality One.

Dualism—The Essence of Creation

To achieve unity, we must put the pieces together. To accomplish such an objective, we need to study, know, and realize the essence of creation—namely *dualism*.

The world, as we know it—from the smallest particle to the largest planet—is kept in balance by a law that is based on the balanced dual nature of all things (wholes, units). Without polarized dualities, there would be no creation, i.e. no universe. Among noticeable polarized pairs are: male and female, odd and even, negative and positive, active and passive, yes and no, true and false—each pair represents a different aspect of the same fundamental principle of polarity. And each aspect partakes of the nature of unity and of the nature of duality.

Adam/Atum [see page 31] is the Perfect Person who combines both the male and female principles. The nature of duality is best expressed in the Ancient Egyptian text, known as the *Bremner-Rhind Papyrus*:

> I was anterior to the Two Anteriors that I made, for I had priority over the Two Anteriors that I made, for my name was anterior to theirs, for I made them anterior to the Two Anteriors...

The dual principle in the creation state was expressed in the pair of **Shu** and **Tefnut**. The pair of husband and wife is the characteristic Egyptian way of expressing duality and polarity. This dual nature was manifested in Ancient Egyptian texts and traditions. The most ancient known texts of the Old Kingdom (ca. 4500 years ago), namely the *Unas Funerary (Pyramid) Texts* §1652, express this dual nature:

> ...and though didst spit out as Shu, and didst spit out as Tefnut.

This is a very powerful analogy, because we use the term, *spitting image* to mean *exactly like the origin.*

Tefnut   Shu

In the Ancient Egyptian texts, Shu and Tefnut are described as the ancestors of all the neteru (gods/goddesses) who begat all beings in the universe. All of the Ancient Egyptian accounts of creation exhibit well defined, clearly demarcated stages, as detailed in several Ancient Egyptian texts.

The principle of dualism is also found in our perception of the universe. It seems that there are basically two aspects of the universe: the physical that we can sense, and the metaphysical that we don't see and hear—not because it does not exist but because its frequency is outside the range of what our senses can detect. There is no distinction between a metaphysical state of being and one with a material body, as now accepted in scientific circles, since Einstein's relativity theory—that matter is a form of energy, a coagulation or condensation of energy. As such, the universe is basically a hierarchy of energies, at different orders of density. Our senses are most familiar with *matter*—the densest form of energy.

This matrix of energies came as a result of the initial act of creation and the subsequent effects of the *Big Bang* that created the universe. This matrix consists of an organized hierarchy. Each level of the hierarchy of existence is a theophany—a creation by the consciousness of the level of being above it. The self-contemplation by each stage of existence brings into being each lower stage. As such, the hierarchy of energies is interrelated, and each level is sustained by the level below it. This hierarchy of energies is set neatly into a vast matrix of deeply interfaced natural laws. It is both physical and metaphysical.

Reconciliation of Dualities Into THE ONE (Tying/Untying the Knot)

In order for the mystical seeker to find the Divine Essence, one must progress in the reverse sequence of creation. In other words, the soul's progress in the journey along the Path is the upward movement from the sphere of the manifested created world, by reconstructing/reassembling the pieces into one unit again—as it was prior to the Big Bang that created the world.

As stated in chapter 4, the active faculties of the Perfected Man are the heart and the tongue, and the role of everyone is to use both faculties to unite the dual aspects of the manifested world. This theme permeates Ancient Egypt, whereby both **Heru** and **Tehuti** are depicted in numerous places, performing the symbolic act of uniting *The Two Lands* [see definition of Two Lands (which has nothing to do with areas of Egypt) in the Glossary].

Heru   Tehuti
(Heart)   (Tongue)

To be married is to tie the knot, just like the Ancient Egyptian symbolic rite of uniting *The Two Lands*. Harmonizing the opposites is tying the balanced polarities in a marriage-type form. Everything in Ancient Egypt (and Sufism) is about the marriage of balanced polarities. When apparent opposites are reconciled (through intellect and intuition), the mystical seeker becomes complete, transcends the bounds of ordinary humanity, and becomes immensely powerful. When tying two polarized opposites, the mystic is making the two parts into one. In other words, to tie is to resolve the apparent differences, i.e. to find that opposites are two sides of the same coin. Each pair represents a different aspect of the same fundamental principle of polarity. And each aspect partakes of the nature of unity and of the nature of duality. When the mystical seeker reaches the second level of consciousness, he recognizes the dual principle in everything in the universe. An example is to find the male and female aspects in each one of us, and learn to harmonize/reconcile them.

The third and final level of consciousness is reached when the mystical seeker finds that the dual nature of a thing is the thing itself—the Two are One. The simplest illustration of this level is the example of a male/female pursuing each's beloved. One appears to be the hunter and the other is the hunted. This is an artificial polarity. In reality, there is no polarity because the hunter is the hunted and both of them are the hunt—the perfect trinity (hunt, hunter, hunted). As the saying goes, *"I chased him until he caught me".*

Other examples of harmonizing/reconciling apparent opposites are to find out that there is no distinction between:

- Sacred and mundane—a good example is the saying, *"one reaps what one sows"*. On a mundane level, it describes the farming process. On a sacred level, it means that good deeds will result in fruitful results. In reality, there is no difference between sacred and mundane interpretations.

- Physical and metaphysical—to *see* a thing (with eyesight) and to *see* what the same thing signifies (with intellect and intuition).

- Inner and outer realities—to discover how the human being is a miniature universe, and that all the powers that operate in the universe are also operating within each one of us. The essence of the Egyptian mystical progression is based on the premise that man is the microcosm in which all attributes are united. [See *Egyptian Divinities: The All Who Are THE ONE*, by same author.]

Knowledge by Spiritual Revelation (Zikr)

As discussed in chapter 2, the Egyptian mystic utilizes both intellect and intuition to gain knowledge of the nature, attributes and works of God. Knowledge through intellect alone is not enough, because of the limitation of our senses.

Egyptian mysticism is a particular method of approach to Reality, which trains and makes use of intuitive and emotional spiritual faculties that are generally dormant and latent. This training aims at dispersing the veils that hide the self from the Real and thereby become transformed or absorbed into the undifferentiated Unity.

The main spiritual realization practice by the Egyptian mystical seekers (Sufis) is called *zikr*, and its purpose is to close the gap between the physical realm/nature and the metaphysical nature. This mystical practice allows the participants the opportunity to achieve knowledge of God by way of revelations. States of visionary ecstasy are brought on by groups of purified mystical seekers, participating in a unified performance/exercise of chanting religious texts, rhythmic dancing, and deep breathing. The goal is to free oneself from the body and to be lifted into the presence of the higher realms of God. In such an ecstatic state, mystical knowledge will flow into the participant mystical seeker unimpeded. As a result, the heart becomes illuminated with "Reality"—the true nature of God. [Detailed information about *zikr* in Appendix C.]

Zikr was introduced into Islamized Sufism by the Egyptian, Dhu 'l-Nun al-Misri, who said, *"zikr is absence from one-self [by recollecting God alone]"*. The absence from oneself is the ideal recollection of God. The whole of Egyptian mysticism rests on the belief that when the individual self is lost, the Universal Self is found. This ecstatic trance of absence from one's self is called *"intoxication"* and the ecstatics are called *"spiritual drunkards"*. The drunkenness of the mystics describes the ecstatic frame of mind in which the spirit is intoxicated with the contemplation of God—just as the body is intoxicated with wine.

By virtue of communications with the Above, as a result of practicing *zikrs*, advanced Egyptian mystics acquire such powers as telepathy, prescience, and miraculous transportation from one place to another.

The ecstatic experience that results from practicing the zikr allows the seeker to go beyond the limitations of his senses—to have a birds-eye view of the world, where he is able to find certain knowledge, patterns, meanings, etc. After the *zikr* practice, the seeker comes back down to earth to utilize his newfound knowledge by using his intellect in more efficient ways to put the pieces together.

Each practice of *zikr* provides new illumination(s), which enables the mystical seeker to utilize his intellect/reason even further, to realize the totality of the universe. Gaining knowledge is a continuous process of using both faculties of intellect and intuition, to interact and enrich one another.

It should be emphasized that in the Egyptian model of mysticism, gaining knowledge (via intellect and intuition) must be channeled into a continuing service in the society. Both knowledge and acts are aspects of a single progressive development along the Spiritual Path.

The second level of consciousness is reached when the mystical seeker comes to realize that the source of all deeds/actions is one source. To use the metaphor of a puzzle, the second level is reached when the mystical aspirant is able to find and reassemble all the different pieces of the cosmic puzzle. Now the picture is complete, but the lines separating the pieces are still visible in his consciousness.

Unification and Deification

The third and final level of consciousness is reached only when the mystical seeker sees the multiplicity in the universe as one indistinguishable Unity. In other words, when the mystical seeker sees the whole picture of the cosmic puzzle as one unit, with no lines/distinctions separating the pieces. This state is reached when the mystic is able to reconcile all dualities and feels no distinction between modes, adjuncts, relations and aspects, i.e. they have all melted together in his consciousness. As a result, the mystic himself becomes melted/annihilated/absorbed/immersed into the Divine Essence. Immersed in Unity, he knows not any form of phenomenal being. The successful mystical seeker has therefore achieved genuine inner unity and wholeness.

The mystical seeker at this stage has accomplished the ultimate goal of the Egyptian mystics, described as the inner marriage of self and soul. In Ancient Egyptian terms, it is the inner marriage of the **Ba** (soul) and the **Ka** (self).

Ba is usually translated as the *soul*. It is the divine, immortal essence. When the **Ba** departs, the body dies. The **Ba** is usually portrayed as a stork with a human head, which is the opposite of the normal depiction of **neteru** (gods/goddesses) as human bodies with animal heads—in other words, as the divine aspect of the terrestrial.

Ka is the spiritual entity that is often translated as the *personality*. The **Ka** does not die with the mortal body. The **Ka** is portrayed as a pair of arms outstretched towards heaven—yearning to unite with the **Ba**.

In love terms, this inner marriage of the **Ba** and **Ka** is similar to the state when the lover, beloved, and their love join to become one—the sea of love. It is the Trinity in One— The Love Triangle. This state of love unity is found in the Ancient Egyptian term, **MiR**, which means both *sea* and *love*. The successful mystic becomes the **Mir**—the *Beloved Holy Sea*.

Pir: The Power House

When the mystic is melted into the Divine Essence, he becomes the Perfected Person, or the Universal Succor, to whom all resort for aid. The ultimate constituents of all existences are drawn towards him, just as iron is drawn to a magnet—and as such he is called *kutb* (meaning *magnetic pole*). The world of sense is subdued by his might and he does what he wills by his power. This power house is called a **Pir**, an Ancient Egyptian term meaning *shrine/spiritual embodiment*.

The unification of the **Ba** (soul) and **Ka** (self) and their melting into the Divine **Ra** (the Creator) produces a powerful trinity—known as **Ba-Ra-Ka**, a transferrable quality of personal blessedness and spiritual force (almost a physical force), which allows the **Pir/Mir** to perform miraculous acts, exemplary human insight, and influence and predict future events. The manifestation of this supernatural power is called **Ka-ra-ma-at/Ka-ra-mat** (or **Ka-ra-maa**), which is an Ancient Egyptian term:

Ka =	the (magnetic) personality of the **Pir/Mir**
Ra =	the Creator (his secret name is **Amen**)
Maat/Maa =	*netert* (goddess) of balance/harmony

7

The Heavenly Helpers

The Eternal Perfect Servants (The Walis)

The state of melting into the Divine Essence is followed (or alternates) with the state of resurrection back in the phenomenal world, in order to serve others. After having passed away from selfhood, i.e. passing from plurality to unity, one must return to the phenomenal world from which he set out, and manifest unity in plurality.

In the Egyptian model, the spiritual Path consists of three journeys:

1. Ascending—where the aspirant travels from the world of creation to the Divine Source.
2. Reaching and being immersed in the Divine. At this state, the individual I-ness disappears into the Oneness of the Divine.
3. Descending back to the world of manifestation, invested with the attributes of God, to serve—to give it all back through **Ka-ra-ma-at**, to his/her fellow man.

The **Pirs/Mirs** become the intermediaries between the earthly living beings and the supernatural powers in higher realms. It is the duty of **Pirs/Mirs** to use their "magical" powers to serve others, during and after their earthly existence.

They are lovingly called **Walis**. This word is used in various senses, derived from its root meaning of *nearness*, e.g. next of kin, patron, godfather, protector, friend—whose holiness brings them near to God, and who receive from Him, as tokens of His peculiar favor, miraculous gifts (**Ka-ra-ma-at**).

After his death, a **Wali** often becomes the patron and protector of the locality or social group in which he lived. Academic Egyptologists describe these **Walis** as *local* or *minor gods*.

Unlike the saints among Christians and Islamic Shiites who are chosen by their religious authorities, **Pirs/Mirs/Walis** are chosen by the ordinary Egyptian people, based on their performances and their abilities to influence supernatural forces in order to assist those on earth.

Staying Alive

Traditional Sufism believes that deification is identified with unification (with God). This concept was recognized in Ancient Egyptian transformational 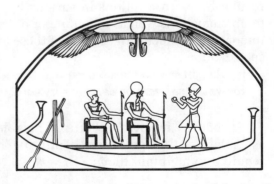 (funerary) texts, where the resurrected pure soul of the **Pir/Mir/Wali**, justified and regenerated, attains a place in the retinue of the **neteru** (gods/goddesses)—the cosmic forces—and eventually takes part in the unceasing round of activity that permits a continued existence of the universe. The role of the **Pir/Mir/Wali**, after his earthly existence, is described in the Ancient Egyptian writing, *becomes a star of gold and joins the company of Ra, and sails with him across the sky in his boat of millions of years.*

The Egyptians (as well as Sufi traditions) recognize that the **Walis** possess unearthly powers that are of the greatest service to mankind. But these powers, if not entirely dependent upon, are greatly reinforced by the pre-

Auset (Isis) giving bread and water to the ba (in the form of a bird).

sentation of the food-and drink offerings, as well as the recitation of incantations, and by performing regular ritual acts, such as sacrifices, libations, communions, dances, and symbolic struggles, which are presently performed by the Egyptian mystics (Sufis) at the various shrines of the **Walis** on a regular basis. Inscriptions in various Egyptian temples and tomb-chapels, as well as in a number of letters, testify to the importance of such rituals. One of these letters, for example, speaks of:

my daughter who makes offerings to the spirit in return for watching over the earthly survivors.

Diodorus, in *Book I, 16*, affirms the role of **Tehuti** (Thoth), as it relates to the significance of offerings and the ordinances required to maintain them:

It was by Tehuti (Hermes), according to the Egyptians, that . . . ., and that ordinances regarding the honors and offerings due to the gods were duly established. . .

Accordingly, Ancient and *Baladi* Egyptians presented/present their deceased with numerous articles of food and drink—at the shrines of the **Pirs/Mirs/Walis**.

The Blessed Shrines (The Ka Houses)

After the earthly death, a **Pir/Mir/Wali's Ba-ra-ka** (spiritual force/blessing) is thought to increase and to inhere in the persons and particularly the places associated and chosen by him. The **Pir/Mir/Wali** chooses and conveys the places for his shrines to his family and friends, during dreams (possibly awake also). As a result, a shrine (or more—usually more than two) is set apart for him/her. Such shrines, in most cases, are not their tombs. The shrines are always selected by the **Pirs/Mirs/Walis** near specific trees, which become a type of sacred grove/garden. The descendants of the **Wali** frequently serve as custodians of the shrines, to make them available to the visiting public, free of charge. These custodians are called *Servants of the **Ka***.

As stated earlier [see page 64], the **Ka** is the essence of the person. Everyone leaves a part of himself (**Ka**) in everything he comes into contact with. Therefore, each shrine contains a relic(s) from the **Pir/Mir/Wali** that he chose himself.

The **Wali's** shrine is usually a small, square, whitewashed building, crowned with a dome-shaped roof that represents the shape of the sky and the Ancient Egyptian symbol for **Neb** (meaning *gold*). The dome sits directly over a mostly empty vault, an oblong monument of stone or brick or wood or copper, usually covered with silk or linen, and surrounded by a railing or screen, of wood or bronze, called *maksoorah*.

When the **Pir/Mir/Wali** dies, his **Ba** (represented by the bird) separates from his **Ka** (his image/personage). To keep the **Ba** and the **Ka** of the **Wali** close to each other, people must visit the shrines and provide offerings on specified weekdays and annual occasions. Egyptians speak of their deceased as living, which shows how definite a belief it is that the soul of the deceased return to their shrines on the specified days of their weekly and annual visitations.

While the shrine houses the **Wali's Ka** (a relic of his choice), his spirit—**Ba** (shown as a bird)—is nearby. The depicted Ancient Egyptian illustration of the tomb/shrine of **Hau** shows the dome-roofed shrine with a sacred tree next to it. Note the depicted bird on the top of the tree. Over the bird is written, *Soul of Ausar.*

Everyone, after leaving the earthly realm, is equated to **Ausar** (Osiris), and as such, the **Ba** represents the soul of any deceased person.

The visitation of shrines is a very common practice among Ancient and *Baladi* Egyptians. People came/come to **Walis'** shrines to ask for blessing, healing, and the goods of this life such as marriage and children and prosperity. Most of the Egyptians not only expect a blessing to follow their visiting the shrine of the folk saint, but they also dread that some misfortune will befall them if they neglect this act. At the shrines, they touch or kiss the holy place, make small gifts or sacrifices, celebrate seasonal festivals, and mark the rejuvenation day(s) of the folk saint, commonly known as *mouled/moulid/mawlid*. The term *mouled* is literally translated as *birthday*—implying a date of renewal/rejuvenation, and has nothing to do with anyone's biological birthday. Many of the **Walis** have several *mouleds* a year.

On these special occasions (*mouleds*), the **Pir/Mir/Wali** becomes an active participant. The ("deceased") **Pir/Mir/Wali** plays an important role in the religious and cosmological framework/operation. The hierarchy of the **Walis** (folk saints) upholds the order of the universe.

[More about the *mouleds* in the following chapters.]

Part
III

The Public Visitation Fairs

8

The Cyclical Renewal Festivals

The Need for Renewal

The Egyptians continued their ancestors' traditions of venerating their folk saints (Pirs/Mirs/Walis) and visiting the shrines during their annual festivals. The aim of the Egyptian festivals was (and continues to be) the rejuvenation and renewal of the cosmic energies.

The main theme of the Ancient Egyptian texts is the cyclical nature of the universe and the constant need for the renewal of such cycles, through well designated festivals.

The Egyptians viewed/view these festivals as part of human existence, which constitutes the rhythm of the life of the community and the individual. This rhythm results from the order of cosmic life.

The renewal and rejuvenation of the life of the cosmos, of the community, and of the individual are effected by rites. These rites had/have the power to bring about the rejuvenation and rebirth of divine life. As such, the Ancient (and present-day) Egyptian festivals came to have the function of enactments of cosmological (religious) renewals.

During the numerous Ancient Egyptian religious festivals, the participants fall back on the archetypal truth of their cosmic consciousness—*As above so below, and as below so above*. Every holy festival actualizes the archetypal holy cycle. These holy cycles have become part of the calendar. More accurately, the calendar served to indicate when the cosmological powers (**neteru**/gods) were manifested, and their renewal cycles. All early Greek and Roman writers affirmed this Ancient Egyptian tradition, such as Plutarch, in his *Moralia*, Vol. V (377,65):

> *. . . They [the Egyptians] associate theological concepts with the seasonal changes in the surrounding atmosphere, or with the growth of the crops and seed-times and plowing. . .*

The present-day name for the annual renewal festival is *mouled/moulid/mawlid*, literally meaning *(renewed) birthday*. *Baladi* Egyptians continue to consider the festivals and their rituals as the climax of their religious practices, which are very critical to the order and harmony of the cosmos—and by extension the well-being of one and all.

All present-day *mouleds* (except for Mohammed's and those of his immediate family) are a continuation of Ancient Egyptian festivals, camouflaged under Islamic names.

The History of Mouleds in Egypt

The annual cyclical festivals (*mouleds*) have been a part of Ancient Egypt's traditions throughout its history. The text on the Palermo Stone (ca. 5000 years ago) gives a list of the principal Ancient Egyptian annual festivals during the next 700 years. Among the listed festivals are the Spring festival of Easter, **Min**, and the **Heb-Sed** festival of the Pharaoh. The

Unas Funerary (Pyramid) Texts of the 5th Dynasty record festive ceremonies that were performed on the 1st, the 6th, and the 15th of every Ancient Egyptian month.

A list of the Ancient Egyptian annual festivals was attempted by the Egyptologist, Schott. It is clear from this list that regular rejuvenation festivals were very common. The temple of Medinat Habu, in Western **Ta-Apet** (Thebes), lists celebrations that were held on 162 days in a year, and took place during several successive days of each month. Some of these celebrations were even repeated in honor of different deities every day during some months. The texts from the temples at Dendera, Edfu, Philae and Esna show many festivals. These lists of festivals in various temple locations are not by any means exhaustive, as they only refer to festivals that had a certain significance in these temples.

In addition to temple festivals, there were also numerous cyclical festivals at the noble/**Pir/Mir/Wali** shrines. A text from the 6th Dynasty (ca. 2300 BCE), reads as follows:

A **coming-forth-unto-the-voice** (meaning the rise/wake) for him in his **tomb-chapel at the monthly and half-monthly festival, on the firsts of the [three] seasons, the firsts of the [twelve] months, and the firsts of the weeks.**

A classic example of the rules and regulations of the festivals, related to the folk saints/**Walis'** veneration, are the ten texts found in Asyut, which are attributed to Hepzefi during the time of Sesostris I (c. 2000 BCE). The texts detail activities that are exactly the same as in present-day *mouleds* in Egypt. [More about these texts in chapter 10.]

The Islamized academia claim that the *mouleds* began in Egypt in the 10th century CE. Historical records prove that they began thousands of years earlier. The Islamic rule (post 641 CE) of Egypt forced people to give Islamic names to ancient traditions. [Read more about it in Appendix B, *Sleeping with the Enemy (Surviving Islam)*.]

The similarities between ancient and present traditions indicate that the modern ceremonies (called *mouleds*) are pre-Christian and pre-Islamic in origin, and are direct ritualistic survivals from the earliest period of Egyptian history.

The official annual number of *mouleds* in present-day Egypt, even though it is contrary to Islam, is estimated at more than 3,000. There is not a single day in Egypt without a *mouled* somewhere, and the participation is very profound. For example, just the three main festivals of the Sidi Ahmed el-Badawi, at the city of Tanta, attract almost as many visitors as Mecca does pilgrims from the whole of the Islamized world. The major Autumn *mouled* of el-Badawi is attended by more than two million people and each of the other two *mouleds* are attended by more than one million visitors. All this is indicative of the *Baladi* Egyptian mystics' adherence by the millions to their ancient traditions.

The Festival Regulators (Auset and Ausar)

The concept of **Ausar** (Osiris) and **Auset** (Isis) was the Egyptian model used to explain all facets of knowledge, as was noted by all early Greek and Roman historians. That concept was also utilized for setting the dates, natures, and objectives of each festival. [See details in chapter 9.]

The most significant (but not the only) aspect of **Auset** (Isis) and **Ausar** (Osiris) is best described by Diodorus of Sicily, *Book I* (11, 5-6), as follows:

> *These two neteru (gods), they hold, regulate the entire universe, giving both nourishment and increase to all things by means of a system of three seasons which complete the full cycle through an unobservable movement. . . .*

This concept was affirmed by Plutarch in his *Moralia*

Vol V (377, 65), as follows:

They [the Egyptians] associate theological concepts with the seasonal changes in the surrounding atmosphere, or with the growth of the crops and seed-times and plowing; as examples the Egyptians say that Osiris is being buried at the time when the grain is sown and covered in the earth and that he comes to life and reappears when plants begin to sprout. For this reason also it is said that Isis, when she perceived that she was pregnant, put upon herself an amulet on the sixth day of the month Phaophi; and about the time of the winter solstice she gave birth to Harpocrates, imperfect and premature, amid the early flowers and shoots. For this reason they bring to him as an offering the first-fruits of growing lentils, and the days of his birth they celebrate after the spring equinox.

Setting the Dates (Rejuvenation Cycles)

From the records of early historians, such as Plutarch, Herodotus and Diodorus, as well as the hundreds of festival records throughout Ancient Egypt, it is clear that setting the dates of these festivals was synchronized with cosmological rhythms. Setting the dates of both ancient and present-day festivals were/are subject to three cycles, individually or a combination of two or all three. The three cycles are:

1. The solar cycle that commands the seasons with all that that implies. The Egyptians developed and followed the Sothic calendar, which is associated with **Auset** (Isis), representing the solar principle in the universe. [See *Egyptian Cosmology: The Animated Universe*, by same author, for details.]

    Since the Islamic occupation of Egypt (641 CE), this calendar is known as the "Coptic" calendar, even though it was developed thousands of years befor Christianity. [See Appendix E for details on the Egyptian calendar.]

2.   The lunar cycle that governs fertility and other biological periodicities, as well as the various meteorological phenomena.

Many of the Ancient Egyptian and present-day *mouleds* were/are celebrated at (or in conjunction with) the new or the full moon. The lunar principle in the universe is represented by **Ausar** (Osiris), who was called *Ausar the Moon*.

3.   The day of the week, which is related to the seven planets and the seven musical notes [also see page 136].

The relationship between the seven days of the week and the seven harmonic natural sounds of the diatonic scale was instituted by the Ancient Egyptians. Such a relationship was a consequence of the heavenly music of the seven (wandering) planets. Dio Cassius (2nd century CE) in his volumes *Roman History* (Book XXXVII, Section 18), stated:

> *The custom of referring the days to the seven stars called planets was instituted by the Egyptians. . .*
> *. . .and to them already an ancestral tradition. . .*

As a consequence of the relationship between the weekdays and the musical harmonies, the vast majority of Ancient (and present-day) Egyptian festivals extend for an octave-week, i.e. 8 days.

As a consequence of utilizing a combination of the three cycles, many festival dates may vary widely from year to year—just like the Easter celebration, which is also determined according to the three Egyptian elements: a weekday that follows a full moon, which follows the vernal equinox (i.e. solar cycle). We therefore must recognize that shown

festival dates in Ancient Egyptian buildings indicate dates
at a specific year(s). Consequently, we occasionally find different dates for the same festival, in different years—just as
we similarly have a different date for Easter every year.

The annual calendar of the Egyptian cyclical festivals
(*mouleds*) determine each's date(s), function(s), and the related venerated deities/Walis to each occasion. The intent is
to synchronize our mode of communication (*as below*) with
the various cyclical patterns in the universe (*so above*).

Some significant points about the Egyptian cyclical calendar of events (past or present) include:

• The calendar is compiled by a few specialists who know
  the significant pattern and cycle of each festival. Just
  like in our present times, only a few people know how
  to set the date for Easter—in Egypt it is/was likewise.
  This is confirmed in Herodotus, *Book Two* (58-59):

  > *It was the Egyptians too who originated, and taught the
  > Greeks to use ceremonial meetings, processions, and pro-
  > cessional offerings: a fact which can be inferred from the
  > obvious antiquity of such ceremonies in Egypt, compared
  > with Greece, where they have been only recently introduced.
  > The Egyptians meet in assembly not once a year only, but
  > on a number of occasions. **There is a sacred tradition
  > which accounts both for the date and for the manner of
  > these observances.** . . .*

• There are several related festivals (*mouleds*) that are observed in certain cyclical sequences, and as such are separated by a set period. Some festivals are spaced at specific cycles—such as 7, 40 or 50 days from other more
  prominent events. Each of these cycles has its own significance. A comparable example in the Christian ecclesiastical calendar is Easter, which is tied to Lent, Ascension Day, and Pentecost.

- The most common example in Egypt of the 7-day cycle is the relationship of many festivals to those of Sidi el-Badawi of Tanta. Many festivals follow Badawi's three annual festivals, exactly a week later.

- The 40-day cycle signifies the time to die or to be re-born. The Egyptians believe that it takes 40 days to die (prior to actual death) and 40 days (after actual death) for the soul to leave the body completely. Consequently, the mummification (body dehydration) period lasted 40 days.

- 50 days is associated with renewal. This was illustrated in the Ancient Egyptian model story when **Set** (Seth), after disposing of **Ausar** (Osiris), ruled as a tyrant for 50 "days" before **Set** was replaced by **Heru** (Horus)—representing the resurrection/renewal of **Ausar**.

- There were/are several nativities for the same occasion/ **neter**, to correspond to several related cycles in the year that are/were associated with the **neter/netert** (god/goddess) or **Wali**. Such a point was noted by Plutarch, in *Moralia* V (372, 52B):

  > . . . . *as is written in the records entitled the **Birthdays** (plural) **of Horus***.

  This tradition continues in our present times where, for example, Sidi el-Badawi of Tanta has three major festivals annually. Most other **Walis** have two or more festivals at one or several shrines.

- Every location/region had/has certain holy days peculiarly consecrated to their patrons, in addition to those common to the regions beyond each locality.

- Festivals usually last one week and a day. Most *mouleds* vary in their beginning weekday, but many begin on a

Friday, and end on the afternoon of the next Friday. The typical eight day duration is consistent with Ancient Egyptian traditions. Musically, the renewal theme of eight terms corresponds to the octave because it reaches through all eight intervals of the scale (the eight white keys of the keyboard).

For example, an octave can be two successive C's (*Do's*) on a musical scale, as illustrated herein on the keyboard.

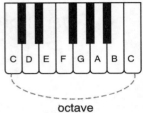

octave

Eight is the number of **Tehuti** (*Hermes* to the Greeks, *Mercury* to the Romans), and at **Khmunu** (Hermopolis), **Tehuti** is called the *Master of the City of Eight*.

Every day has its peculiar activities and each tetrachord (4 days) has its own energy theme.

The eve of the last day of the octave-week festival is called the *Great Night/Evening*—it is the climax of the festival [as will be detailed in chapter 10].

•   It is important to remember that all Egyptian *mouleds* (except for those assigned to Mohammed and his family) follow the Ancient Egyptian solar calendar, and not the Islamic purely lunar reckoning.

•   The Islamic names of the Egyptian *mouleds* are a sheer facade to protect and maintain ancient traditions.

•   Sunset marks the beginning of the day in Ancient and *Baladi* (Sufi) traditions. As such, an apparent discrepancy of one day between Egyptian dates and the adopted Western reckoning is possible in some festival dates [shown in the next chapter].

9

Samples of Ancient-Present Festivals

Familiar Festivals

The following is a sample of familiar Ancient-present Egyptian festivals, showing their dates, nature, and traditions.

The sample festivals show/confirm:

1. The cyclical patterns stated in the previous chapter.
2. The Egyptian connectivity between the cyclical cosmological patterns and earthly activities.
3. The conceptual role of **Ausar** (Osiris) and **Auset** (Isis) in the Egyptian festivals. [Also see page 76.]
4. That Ancient Egyptian festivals are continued in present-day *mouleds*.
5. That the Christian annual festivals are an adoption of Ancient Egyptian festivals.

The dates provided in the sample festivals are based on the Ancient Egyptian calendar (which is still in use under the name *Coptic Calendar*), as well as the equivalent date in the Latin calendar. [See Appendix E: The Egyptian vs. Latin Calendar.]

The Egyptian Calendrical New Year's Day

The Egyptian calendrical New Year's Day currently corresponds to 11 September of the Latin calendar.

Not coincidentally, the ecclesiastical year that is followed by the Orthodox churches, according to Byzantine practice, like Ancient Egypt, also begins in the month of September.

The Wag Festival

The last day of the Ancient Egyptian *Wag Festival* was celebrated, according to Plutarch [*Moralia* Vol V (378,68)], on the 19th of **Toot** (27 September). It was common for those who attended to greet each other with expressions like, *"How sweet a thing is truth!"*, or *"The tongue is fortune, the tongue is God!"*.

This festival signifies that the River Nile has risen to its greatest height, or nearly so. **Ausar** (Osiris) respresents the rising water. **Ausar** is also known as the *Manifester of Truth*—hence, the Egyptians said, *"How sweet a thing is truth!"* The second sentence relates to **Tehuti** (Thoth), whose symbol was/is the tongue. Hence the Egyptians said, *"The tongue is fortune, the tongue is God!"*

Tehuti

The same festival/*mouled* continues to be celebrated to date, camouflaged in a Christian/Islamic pretense. Some call it the *Cross,* or *Mar Barsoum el Elryan Festival,* or *Mohammed Barsoom Festival/Mouled.*

☞ **100 days later is the Eve of 6 January—the Epiphany/Rebirth of Ausar as the renewed Heru.**

The Conception (Planting) Mouled

In the typical Egyptian story form, forty days after
Auset's (Isis') birthday [see last page in this chapter], i.e. 6 Babeh/
Phaophi (17 October), Auset was impregnated with Ausar's
seed. Accordingly, Ancient (and present-day) Egyptians
planted seeds throughout Egypt on this date, in a special
mouled with special rituals to ensure a successful harvest.

Planting is the burying of seed into earth. As such, planting is associated with burial—death that leads to a resurrection, i.e. sprouting. This beautiful analogy was described by
Plutarch, in his *Moralia* Vol V (377, 65), where we read:

> . . . *the Egyptians say that Osiris is being buried at the time
> when the grain is sown and covered in the earth and that he
> comes to life and reappears when plants begin to sprout. For
> this reason also it is said that Isis, when she perceived that
> she was pregnant, put upon herself an amulet on the sixth day
> of the month Phaophi* [equivalent to 17 October in the Latin
> calendar]. . . .

Ausar (Osiris) represents the process, growth, and the
underlying cyclical aspects of the universe—the principle that
makes life come from apparent death. The most impressive
representation of the concept of regeneration, namely Ausar,
is the illustration depicting Ausar with 28 stalks of wheat
growing out of his coffin. [See illustration on page 87.]

On this very prominent day, present-day Egyptians com-
memorate one of three major annual *mouleds* of Sidi el-
Badawi in Tanta, where the official attendance is more than
two million people.

**☞ 40 days after planting the seeds, the Egyptians
celebrated/celebrate the event of the Last Supper
and the Loss of Ausar (Osiris).**

The Last Supper (Darkness Overtakes Light)

Forty days after the burial of **Ausar's** (Osiris') seeds into Mother Earth—**Auset** (Isis)—**Ausar** met his demise. In the typical Ancient Egyptian story form, Plutarch writes in his *Moralia*, Vol. V (356, 13), about how **Ausar** was invited by **Set** (Seth) to a feast where **Set** and his accomplices tricked **Ausar** into laying down in a makeshift coffin. Plutarch continues with...

> . . . . *and those who were in the plot ran to it and slammed down the lid, which they fastened by nails from the outside and also by using molten lead. Then they carried the chest to the river and sent it on its way to the sea through the Tanitic Mouth. Wherefore the Egyptians even to this day name this mouth the hateful and execrable. Such is the tradition. They say also that the date on which this deed was done was the* **17*th* day of Athor** [27 November]**, when the sun passes through Scorpion**.

The events of 17 **Hatoor**/Athor (27 November), as reported by Plutarch, have all the elements of the biblical Jesus' Last Supper, i.e. a conspiracy, feast, friends, and betrayal. However, for the Ancient Egyptians, there are other meanings to the story. Plutarch, in *Moralia* Vol V (366, 39D), wrote:

> **The story told of the shutting up of Osiris in the chest seems to mean nothing else than the vanishing and disappearance of water**. . . . *at the time when. . . . the Nile recedes to its low level and the land becomes denuded.* **As the nights grow longer, the darkness increases, and the potency of the light is abated and subdued**. . . .

The antagonistic relationship between **Ausar** (Osiris) and **Set** (Seth)—as it relates to environmental conditions—is mentioned by Plutarch, *Moralia* Vol V (364, 33B), as such:

> . . . *The Egyptians simply give the name of Ausar* [Osiris]

to the whole source and faculty creative of moisture, believing this to be the cause of generation and the substance of life-producing seed; and the name of Set [Typhon in Greek] they give to all that is dry, fiery, and arid, in general, and antagonistic to moisture. . . .

. . . The insidious scheming and usurpation of Set [Typhon], then, is the power of drought, which gains control and dissipates the moisture which is the source of the Nile and of its rising. . . .

Set (Seth)   Ausar (Osiris)

The *Loss of **Ausar*** (Osiris) is now celebrated in the *Abu Sefein Mouled* at the same time and with the same traditions, i.e. a big feast followed by to a 40-day cycle of figurative death—by fasting and other disciplinary means.

☞ **28 days after the Last Supper is the birth/rebirth of the renewed king on 25 December.**

☞ **40 days after the Last Supper is Epiphany.**

The Advent of Ausar (Osiris)

Ausar's (Osiris') life, being a symbol of the moon, is associated with a cycle of 28 days (4 weeks). This was echoed later in the Christian Advent, which in Latin is *ad-venio*, meaning *to come to*. The *Catholic Encyclopedia* admits that: *"Advent is a period embracing 4 Sundays. The first Sunday may be as early as 27 November, and then Advent has 28 days."* As noted above, 27 November is the date of the symbolic *Last Supper*, *Death*, and *Loss of **Ausar***.

The 28-day cycle of Ausar and its relationship to the regeneration principle is nicely depicted in the famed scene of the resurrection of the wheat, which depicts Ausar with 28 stalks of wheat growing out of his coffin.

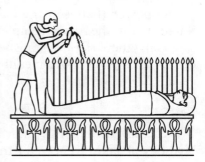

The ecclesiastical year begins with Advent in the Western churches. According to the *Catholic Encyclopedia*, *"the faithful are admonished, during this time:*

- *To prepare themselves worthily to celebrate the anniversary of the Lord coming into the world as the incarnate God of love,*

- *Thus to make their souls fitting abodes for the Redeemer coming in Holy Communion and through grace, and*

- *Thereby to make themselves ready for His final coming as judge, at death and at the end of the world."*

All the above elements are of Ancient Egyptian origin. Such traditions were observed during (and in fact were based on) the annual jubilee of the Ancient Egyptian King, known as the Sed (or Heb-Sed) Festival, which was always held during the month of Kee-hek (Khoiakh, i.e. December) every year. This festival dates from time immemorial, and continued to be celebrated throughout the Ancient Egyptian history.

The intent of this annual event was the renewal/rejuvenation of the supernatural powers of the King. The renewal rituals aimed at bringing new life force to the King, i.e. a (figurative) death and a (figurative) rebirth of the reigning King. In the Ancient Egyptian traditions, this concept of perpetual power (between the old and the new) is eloquently illustrated in the **Ausar** Temple at **Abtu** (Abydos) [as shown on page 143], where **Heru** is being born out of **Ausar**, after **Ausar's** death. This gives more meaning to the phrase: *The King is dead—Long live the King.*

In the Ancient Egyptian traditions, the rejuvenation/birthday of a new/renewed King comes symbolically 28 days after 27 November—the symbolic *Last Supper* and the *Death of Ausar*—i.e. 25 December. The Christian calendar celebrates the same day as the birth (rebirth) of the new King, namely Jesus, who is referred to as a *King* throughout the Bible. The 28-day cycle signifies the Advent (both in Ancient Egyptian and Christian traditions) of the *King*. [For more information about Jesus as a King, see *Tut-Ankh-Amen: The Living Image of the Lord*, by same author.]

All the elements mentioned in the *Catholic Encyclopedia* on the previous page concur with their Egyptian origin, whereby **Ausar** (Osiris) incarnates as **Heru** (Horus), and that **Ausar** is the judge of the dead. [Also see page 132.]

Due to the absolute lack of historical and archeological evidence to support the biblical accounts of Jesus' birth, life, and death, and in order for the Christian church to set a birth date of some kind, they turned to Egypt. Practically all churches picked their dates from an Ancient Egyptian list, which was attributed to Clement of Alexandria. The list places several dates: 25 Pachon (20 May), 24 or 25 Pharmuthi (19 or 20 April). Clement however indicated that Epiphany, and with it probably the Nativity, was celebrated on 15 or 11 of Tobi (10 or 6 January). 6 January is proven to be the date adopted for his "birthday" throughout the various churches in the Mediterranean Basin. 25 December came later and was based on the Julian calendar, which is 13 days behind 6 January. [See explanation of the 13-day difference in Appendix E.]

The King's New Year's Day (January 1)

As noted earlier, the typical Egyptian festivals extend for an octave-week. As such, the Egyptian King's renewal day of 25 December (Julian calendar) has its climax in its octave (8 days later) on 1 January—the New Year's Day for the rejuvenated King. On the 22nd of **Kee-hek**/Khoiakh (1 January), during the annual jubilee festivities, a special ceremony was held, at which a ceremonial voyage was led by the effigy of **Ausar** (Osiris), accompanied by 34 images of divinities in 34 little boats illuminated by 365 candles—the candles representing the number of days in a regular year.

Epiphany (January 6)

A cycle of forty days after the Egyptian Last Supper (27 November) and the death of **Ausar** (Osiris) was/is the Epiphany on 6 January, which was later adopted in the Christian calendar of events for the same objective.

Like the Ancient Egyptian traditions, the original intent of Epiphany in the Eastern Church is for one about to be baptized—the sacrament of Baptism. As stated earlier, baptism represents figurative death and rebirth. A born-again cycle typically takes 40 days (from 27 November to 6 January). At the end of the cycle, the people bathe in the Nile (baptism), and the fast is broken. Happy days are here again.

Baladi Egyptians (who were forced to be Moslems) continue to celebrate this occasion because it is an Ancient Egyptian tradition that was later adopted by the Christians.

The Islamic Egyptian government has restored this special day as a national holiday in 2003—unaware of its Ancient Egyptian origin.

Lent

Lent denotes the 40 days' fast that precedes the Holy Week of Easter. One has to (figuratively) die in order to be (figuratively) reborn. Lent represents the figurative death (fasting, self-discipline, etc) before rebirth.

Lent and Easter pre-date Christianity, as explained below. Lent was, in origin, the time of the final preparation for candidates for the solemn rite of baptism at the Easter Vigil. The ritual of baptism was performed in the sacred lakes of the Ancient Egyptian temples and in the River Nile itself.

Easter

It has been common knowledge that the Christian Easter was not an historical event, but that the festival pre-existed Christianity. The Webster's dictionary describes Easter as the *"name of pagan vernal festival almost coincident in date with paschal festival of the church"*. The so-called *"pagan"* festival is the Egyptian Easter. In the Egyptian (and later the Christian) calendar, Easter is the center of the greater part of the ecclesiastical year—from Septuagesima to the last Sunday after Pentecost, the feast of the Ascension, Pentecost, Corpus Christi, and all other movable feasts—because they are tied to the Easter date.

Commemorating Easter is the cornerstone upon which the Christian faith is built. Yet the Apostolic Fathers do not mention it because it was a continuation of an existing Jewish holiday—namely Passover—which in turn was/is an adoption of an Ancient Egyptian Spring festival.

Ancient Egyptian records indicate that the Egyptian

Spring Festival was in existence at least since the Old Kingdom. The purpose of such festival was/is the renewal of nature in the springtime, when life returns once more to the world.

As stated earlier, **Ausar** (Osiris) represents the cyclical nature of the universe, the principle that makes life come from apparent death. It was therefore natural that **Ausar** be identified with Spring—of the day when he was believed to have risen from the dead.

Ausar

The Easter celebration, like all Egyptian festivals, lasts an octave-week (known in the Christian calendar as the Holy Week—extending from Palm Sunday to Easter Sunday). The Ancient Egyptian Holy Week is followed by Easter Monday—known in Egypt as *Sham en Neseem*. This is the only official national holiday that survived since Ancient Egyptian times.

As an extension of the Ancient Egyptian traditions, numerous *mouleds* are held throughout Egypt during the Easter Holy Week by the Egyptian mystics (Sufis). One of these events is the annual (non-Christian) *Mouled of Abu-Hareera*, which is held in Giza.

Ascension Day

In the Ancient Egyptian tradition, the spirit of the deceased takes 40 days to completely depart the body and ascend to the heavens. Accordingly, the mummification (body dehydration) period lasted 40 days. Likewise, the Christian calendar commemorates Ascension Day on the 40th day after Easter, when it celebrates *"the bodily ascent of Jesus into Heaven, on the 40th day after resurrection".*

The First Teardrop

After **Ausar** (biblical Jesus) ascended to the heavens, his wife **Auset** began weeping. The Eve of the 11th of the Ancient Egyptian month of **Ba-oo-neh** (18 June) is called *"Leylet en-Nuktah"* (or the *Night of the Tear Drop*), as it commemorates the first drop that falls into the Nile, to begin the annual flood season. Astrologers calculate the precise moment when the "drop" is to fall, which is always in the course of the night above mentioned. This Ancient Egyptian celebration is recognized in northern Cairo as *Mouled el-Embabi*.

This ancient festival was particularly welcomed by the Egyptian peasants—all along the Nile Valley. Diodorus of Sicily tells us how the husbandmen indulged in recreations of every kind, and showed their gratitude to God for the benefits of the inundation. According to Heliodorus, it was one of the principal festivals of the Egyptians. Libanius asserts that these rites were deemed of so much importance by the Egyptians throughout the land, that unless they were performed at the proper season, and in a becoming manner, by the persons appointed to this duty, they believed that the Nile would refuse to rise and inundate the land.

The Nile begins to rise about, or soon after, the period of the summer solstice. Two weeks after the first teardrop, i.e. from, or about, the 27th of the month **Ba-oo-neh** (3rd of July) the incremental increases in the water level of the Nile were proclaimed daily in the streets of the city, as stated by Plutarch, and were continued by *Baladi* Egyptians until the Aswan High Dam was built in the 1960s.

One of the most compelling parts of the Egyptian Model Story of **Auset** (Isis) and **Ausar** (Osiris) is how these two symbols relate to the flood season in Egypt. The Egyptians associated the beginning of the flood to **Auset** after her husband/soulmate, namely **Ausar**, ascended to heaven 40 days after his death, and then started weeping, begging her dead husband to rise again. Egyptians associated the first teardrop with the beginning of the rise of the Nile. **Auset** continued to weep, wishing for her husband to rise.

Auset   Ausar

The beauty here is that **Auset** is wishing her husband to rise from the dead, and the water of the Nile is consequently rising as well. It should be noted that the water of the Nile is symbolized by **Ausar** himself.

Plutarch described this relationship, in his *Moralia* V (366, 38A), as follows:

> *. . . As the Egyptians regard the Nile as the effusion of Ausar [Osiris], so they hold and believe the earth to be the body of Auset [Isis], not all of it, but so much of it as the Nile covers, fertilizing it and uniting with it. From this union they make Heru [Horus] to be born. . .*

In other words, **Auset** recreates/regenerates **Ausar** from her tears every year. Her tears are blood-red in color, which is the same color of the floodwaters, since this water comes as a result of the rainy season in Ethiopia, which erodes the silt of the Ethiopian highlands, and carries it towards Egypt along the Blue Nile and other tributaries. So, **Auset's** tears represent this reddish color of the water during the flood season. In essence, **Auset** (Isis) is crying a river—so to speak. The Christian faithful follow the same Ancient Egyptian traditions in their presentations of the statues of Mary with bloody teardrops coming out of her eyes.

☞ **It should be noted that from 3 July (the actual beginning of the rise of the Nile) to Assumption Day (22 August) is 50 days—a Pentecost.**

The Egyptian Pentecost

The *Apostles (Prophets) Mouled* in Egypt is held 50 days after Easter. Likewise, in the Christian calendar, the faithful celebrate Pentecost, which happens 50 days after Easter. Pentecost celebrates *"the descent of the Holy Spirit upon the Apostles"*.

This festival is of Ancient Egyptian origin. Pentecost signifies the period of the *Khamaseen* (meaning *the Fifty*), when the southerly hot and reddish sandstorms and winds are of frequent occurrence. This annual event commences on the day immediately following Good Friday, i.e. Easter (Light) Saturday, and ceases on the Day of Pentecost (or Whitesunday)—an interval of 50 days.

This pentecostal event is related to the Ancient Egyptian allegory about **Auset** (Isis) and **Ausar** (Osiris), that after **Ausar** was killed, **Set** (Seth) became the king of Egypt and he ruled oppressively. **Set** represents the color red and the oppressive weather that is dry, fiery, and arid. In essence, Set represents the red, hot cloud of dust—*Khamaseen*.

At the time of his death, **Ausar** and **Auset** had no children, but by mystical and "magical" means, **Ausar** impregnated **Auset**. As a result, **Auset** conceived a son, namely **Heru** (Horus), who was raised secretly in the marshes of the Nile Delta. The allegory continues that as soon as **Heru** (Horus) had grown to manhood, he challenged **Set** for the right to the throne. After several battles between them, they went to the council of the twelve **neteru** (gods) to determine who should rule. The council decided that **Ausar/Heru** should regain the throne of Egypt, and **Set** should rule over the deserts/ wastelands. In weather terms, this decision by the council ended the 50 days of oppressive weather (the *Khamaseen*). The date of judgment by the council of **neteru**/apostles/prophets was declared to be Whitesunday (White-Sunday), meaning the 50 reddish days are over, i.e. it's all clear now.

Transfiguration of Heru (Horus)

Fifty days after **Auset's** (Isis') first teardrop (on 17 June), i.e. on 6 August, the Ancient Egyptians celebrated the reappearance of **Ausar** (Osiris) in the form of the resurrected **Heru** (Horus). This was confirmed by Plutarch in his *Moralia*, Vol. V (372,52B):

> *In the sacred hymns of Osiris they call upon him who is hidden in the arms of the Sun; and on the* **thirtieth of the month Epiphi** [6 August] *they celebrate the birthday of the* **Eyes of Horus**, *at the time when the Moon and the Sun are in a perfectly straight line, since they regard not only the Moon but also the Sun as the eye and light of Horus.*

This is identical with the later Christians' claim of the transfiguration of Jesus, celebrated by the Orthodox church on 6 August. This holiday commemorates the *"revelation of Jesus' divinity to Peter, James, and John"*.

This Ancient Egyptian tradition continues, camouflaged in the *Mouled of El-Desouki*, at the town of Desouk, on the east bank of the westerly branch of the Nile River. El-Desouki is lovingly known as *Abu-el-e-nane* (of the two eyes), just like **Heru** *(Horus) the Elder of the Two Eyes.*

The two eyes of **Heru** (Horus) mentioned by Plutarch are the sun and the moon, symbols of his parents—**Auset** and **Ausar**. As stated on pages 77 and 78, **Auset** (Isis) represents the solar principle in the universe, and **Ausar** (Osiris) represents the lunar principle in the universe.

This *mouled* is recognized by the best magical (divination) acts in Egypt, which corresponds to the later Christian celebration, whose main theme is the "revelation of (Jesus) divinity".

Our Lady Meriam (Assumption of Our Lady Day)

In the typical Egyptian story form, **Auset** (Isis) finished her crying over her soulmate, **Ausar** (Osiris), in about the middle of August, which means that **Auset** has cried all the tears she had. It is at this point in time that the Egyptians (both ancient and modern) hold a festival, signifying the last teardrop from **Auset**, which will cause the peak of the flood level. It is during this celebration that the Egyptians throw an effigy of **Auset** into the waters, to symbolize that **Auset** drowned in her own tears. Incredibly, the church has adopted the same exact date to represent the ascension of the "Virgin Mary" to heaven as Assumption Day, which is defined as:

The dogma of the taking up of the body and soul of the Virgin Mary (Auset is also a virgin) into heavens after her death.

The Orthodox church celebrates Assumption Day on 15 August, which is the same exact day when present-day Egyptians observe the end of the rainy season in Ethiopia.

In addition to the official governmental celebrations, the *Baladi* Egyptians hold a *mouled*, called *Sitena Meriam* (meaning *Our Lady Meriam*). This is not a "Christian festival". The festival lasts the typical Egyptian octave-week (8 days). The last day of the celebration is 16 **Mesoree** (22 August).

Another title for this festival is *Bride of the Nile*—uniting **Auset** with **Ausar** (Osiris). **Auset** has submerged—as a symbol of earth—in her husband's body—symbol of water. This unification is another perfect application of the concept of inner marriage that permeates Ancient Egyptian (and later Sufi) traditions.

☞ **It should be noted that from 3 July (the beginning of the rise of the Nile waters) to 22 August is 50 days—another Pentecost.**

Auset's (Mary's) Birthday

The Ancient Egyptians followed the Sothic year, a period of 365.25636 days [as shown in Appendix E]. Besides the adjustments made for the 0.00636 days per year [see details in Appendix E], the Ancient Egyptians divided the year into 12 equal months of 30 days each, and added five (plus one every 4 years) extra days. These extra days currently begin on 6 September. In the typical Egyptian story form, five **neteru** (gods) were born on each of the five days—**Ausar** (Osiris), **Auset** (Isis), **Set** (Seth), **Heru Behdety** (Apollo), and **Het-Heru** (Hathor).

The Nativity of the Virgin Mary is celebrated in the Orthodox church on the Eve of 8 September, which is **Auset's** (Isis') "birthday" as the second of 5 deities born in the 5 "extra days".

Auset's (Isis) role in the Egyptian Model Story and the biblical story of the Virgin Mary are strikingly similar, for both were able to conceive without male impregnation. **Heru** (Horus) was conceived and born after the death of **Auset's** husband, and, as such, **Auset** was revered as the **Virgin Mother**. [See more details in chapter 12.]

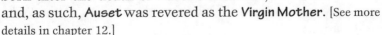 **40 days after Auset's (Mary's) birthday is the Egyptian Conception (Planting) Mouled.**

10

The Egyptian Spirited Fairs (*Mouleds*)

Family Reunion

As noted earlier, the reason for the annual Ancient Egyptian festivals are renewals and rejuvenation of the life of the cosmos. Ancient and *Baladi* Egyptians do not categorize the activities at the festivals as sacred or mundane. As such, the gay and secular side of religious ceremonies is an essential part of the Egyptian festivals. The sports, games, theatres, shadow-plays, coffee booths, beer booths, sweet stalls, eating houses, the meeting of friends, the singing, the dancing, and the laughter, are as much part of a *mouled* as the religious processions and the visits to the shrines of the **Walis** (folk saints).

The *mouled* is a family reunion between the spirits of the past—the **Walis**—and the spirits of the present—the visitors of all ages. The Ancient Egyptian texts and the wall reliefs draw a colorful and graphic picture of the way in which the deceased **Wali** and his visitors met in and near the shrines, which became *houses of the joy of the heart* on that occasion.

According to early writers such as Strabo, people from all classes and ages attended these festivals. Herodotus stated that 700,000 people attended the joyful festival (*mouled*) of **Bast** (Bastet), right outside Zagazig in the Nile Delta.

In addition to the reunion between the **Wali** and the people, the *mouled* allows for other various kinds of reunions, such as:

1. Between the local mystic (Sufi) fellowship and other fellowships. Mystics come from various regions, near and far, to participate in the festivities/ceremonies.

2. Between various people from local, regional, and national regions who attend the *mouled*. Attendees include all family members.

3. Between old friends who have not seen each other for a while.

4. Between old foes who must resolve their animosities and start a renewed friendship in the name of the venerated **Wali**. People forgive past fights/disagreements and start a new page, i.e. the *mouled* reinforces and strengthens the social fabric—it is a societal renewal.

The main objectives of these *mouleds'* attendants are:

1. Visiting the **Wali** at his shrine, in order to participate in the rejuvenation of the cosmic cycles.

2. To acquire a blessing and a friend and intercessor in the heavenly court, by vowing to donate goods or perform a service, on behalf of the **Wali**.

3. To recreate and refresh soul and body, with thankful joy, and to take part in the amusements.

4. To recruit new members for the mystical fellowships.

The Mouleds' Overall Plan of Activities

Early Greek and Roman writers have confirmed the organized and orderly nature of the Ancient Egyptian festivals. Plato adopted the Egyptian model of festivities in *Laws VII* (798e-799b), where he states,

> ATHENIAN: Well, **can any of us find a better device for this purpose than that employed in Egypt?**
> CLINIAS: And what is that?
> ATHENIAN: . . . **First, the festivals must be fixed by compiling an annual calendar to show what feasts are to be celebrated, at what dates, and in honor of what deities, sons of deities, or spirits, respectively.**

> Next, **certain authorities must determine what hymn is to be sung on the feast of each divinity, and by what dances the ceremony of the day is to be graced.** When this has been determined, the whole citizen body must do public sacrifice to the Destinies and the entire pantheon at large, and consecrate each hymn to its respective god or other patron by solemn libation. If any man tries to introduce hymn or dance into the worship of any deity in contravention of these canons, the priests of either sex, acting in conjunction with the curators of law, shall have the warrant both of religion and law in excluding him from the festival;

All the elements and rules governing the Ancient Egyptian festivals, as reported by Plato, are exactly applicable to present-day *mouleds* with organized and detailed schemes.

Such festival traditions were present in Egypt long ago. Hepzefi's tomb from Asyut, dating from the Middle Kingdom (ca. 2000 BCE), contains ten documents specifying:

- The dates of several types of festivities. Some festivals are to be held annually, others are held seasonally, and some festivals are observed centuries apart.

- The course of the procession between different shrines and temples for each festival day, and the activities required at each shrine/temple.

- Activities/actions on every day of the festivities during its octave duration(s), such as performances of specific rituals and recitations, as well as the amounts and types of offerings at each shrine.

- Time of day/night for each ritualistic activity.

- The lighting scheme during the light vigil, and the ritual of kindling the light of torches, which are carried in the procession.

- The festive atmosphere of music, dance, entertainment, games, sports, etc.

The present-day *mouled* is likewise a picturesque ceremony with merry sights and tonic atmosphere, even though all such activities are totally forbidden in Islam. The streets are crowded with happy and orderly people. Streets and shops are gaily decorated and brightly lit.

No two *mouleds* are exactly alike. In general, the primary activities in the Egyptian festivals (*mouleds*) are:

1. The opening ceremonies.
2. Ongoing rituals.
3. Visitation by the public to the shrine.
4. Public offerings.
5. Boy circumcisions (initiations).
6. A variety of booths for food, drinks, etc.
7. Lively entertainment.
8. Lively games and sports.
9. The climactic Octave Eve activities.
10. The closing ceremonies—the Final Procession.

1. The Opening Ceremonies

On the opening day, the present leader of the mystical (Sufi) fellowship that is associated with the celebrated **Wali** leads a special procession towards the shrine of the **Wali**. This leader is frequently a spiritual or blood descendant (or both) of the **Wali**.

The Egyptian term for this procession is *zaffa* or *'urs,* which literally means a *wedding procession*, for the purpose of consummating a marriage. The term, *zaffa*, has a subtle reference to the unitive action—the inner marriage between the self (**Ka**)—the personage of the **Wali**, and his soul (**Ba**). This idea is expressed in Sufi poetry as sexual intercourse and becoming one, and hence the term *zaffa*—a procession to be wed.

The modern concept that the soul (**Ba**) visits the shrine (**Ka**) on specified days conforms to a well-known vignette in *The Book of the Coming Forth by Light/Day* (wrongly known as *The Book of the Dead*), depicting the soul (**Ba**) in the form of a bird, descending the shaft in order to unite with the **Ka** of the deceased. This concept is to be found in Egyptian religious texts of all periods.

The objective of the *zaffa* (procession) is to perform an inaugural ceremony to "awaken" the **Wali** through the inner marriage of his **Ka** (represented in a relic of his choice) and **Ba** (the soul).

The *zaffa* consists of members of the local mystical (Sufi) fellowship, who don't walk, but rather move in rhythmic dancing strides. They are accompanied by musicians, dancers, lantern bearers, incense bearers, etc.

At the head of the *zaffa* is one of the most venerable of the fellowship, playing the Egyptian *nay* (a sort of flute). In

Ancient Egypt, the procession was also usually headed by a flute-player, according to Herodotus. Other members of the fellowship play other musical instruments. In these festivals, music was required in ritual performances, just like modern times, and was, according to Apuleius, of a spiritual character. It was/is called **samaa**, which was/is an Ancient Egyptian term meaning *to unite through sound/music*.

The *zaffa* follows a specific route with specific rituals. It generally takes an average of two hours, but could be much longer. The route typically includes pauses at certain places and shrines in the district for recitations and other rituals at the shrines of the other **Walis** in the district, to heighten the collective energies in the ceremonies. The procession may occasionally be punctuated by special exhibitions of ritual dancing, including the whirling—usually with music, and at night with lanterns and many other illuminating devices.

Ancient Egyptian tombs show choirs of male and female singers approaching the shrine. The female singers wave sistra and necklaces; the male singers mark the measure by clapping their hands. The lord of  the shrine awaits the choirs, which sing songs ending with special recitations.

The local mystical (Sufi) fellowship leads the procession to the shrine and circles it seven times. Then they enter the shrine, purifying it with incense, and reciting certain formulas (spells). In their rituals, these mystical (Sufi) groups connect the past, present, and future through movements, gestures, and facial expressions, in addition to reciting poetry, singing, and dancing. The intent is to facilitate the joining (inner marriage) of the **Wali's Ba** and **Ka**.

As part of the present-day rituals, the choir cries, *"By the power of so-and-so, rise!"*—reminiscent of Ancient Egyptian's term of **prt-r-hrw**, meaning *coming forth*, or a *going up at the voice* of **Heru** (Horus). This phrase mediates the call for the deceased, represented as **Ausar** (Osiris), to resurrect anew as **Heru**, representing the rebirth of **Ausar**. This is the essence of the *mouled*—to rejuvenate and regenerate the old (**Ausar**) into the renewed (**Heru**). [See the Ancient Egyptian depiction of **Heru** rising out of **Ausar** on page 143.]

In Ancient Egyptian, **prt** means *ascent*, *going up to* or *procession to*. The term indicates the intent of meeting souls in higher realms—ascending to them. The name of the ritual given to this ancient rite was **prt-r**, meaning *the coming forth* or *going up*, or *to rise*. The same is used to mean *to rise* of the sun. The call to the **Wali** is, in essence, to *rise and shine*.

The renewal rites at the temple/shrine are the essence of the ritual ceremonies. The words accompanying the action are of even greater significance. The *magic word*, the incantation, actuates the power and endows the ritual acts with a magical religious effect.

The *magic* of the recited word is embodied in two **neteru** (gods), who represent certain aspects of the powers of **Tehuti** (Thoth). The two **neteru** (gods) are:

Hu/Hw [shown herein], who represents the authoritative utterance, and

Sia [shown herein], who represents the mind, consciousness, knowledge, understanding, perception, wisdom, etc.

The combined powers of **Hu/Hw** and **Sia** are represented in Ancient Egypt as **Heka** (Hike). As such, **Heka** [shown herein] represents the ability to transform, by using the right words. The words of power (magical words) are called **Heka-u** (plural of **Heka**). In other words, the right words have powerful transformational (magical) effects.

[More about the power of words/names in Appendix A, pages 138-9.]

The successful rituals of the opening ceremonies result in awakening the **Wali**. A number of celebrations are described in Ancient Egyptian texts in which the "deceased" plays a prominent role during the festival days. Examples are in two tombs at Meir from the Middle Kingdom (ca. 2000 BCE), whereby the occupant stands as if he has just emerged from the underworld, happily receiving a festive group of dancers, musicians, singers and wrestlers, who come to pay homage to him in a procession. Texts next to the depictions read: **for (***i.e. to increase***) your vitality**. Meanwhile a man is depicted presenting offerings and flowers to the deceased. [More about offerings later in this chapter.]

The presentation of a bouquet of flowers to the **Wali** at his shrine was/is intended to utilize the sweet scent of the flowers to renew the **Wali's** life. In Ancient Egyptian texts, there are numerous references to the *sweet scent of the praised ancestors*. In Ancient Egyptian traditions, the **neter** (god), **Nefer-Tum**, represents the perpetual renewed creation, which is the goal of the Egyptian festivals. As such, the rejuvenated **neteru/Walis** were equated to **Nefer-Tum**, who is usually depicted rising out of a blue lotus.

After the opening ceremonies of getting the Wali to rise and shine, the *mouled* is officially open.

2. Ongoing Rituals

The local fellowship that celebrates the annual festival(s) of its founder (Pir/Mir/Wali) is always joined by other mystical (Sufi) fellowships from surrounding areas. The visiting mystical (Sufi) fellowships become more and more visible as the days of the *mouled* progress.

The various Sufi fellowships arrive in processions with their distinguishable banners, insignia, and colors. Each fellowship is accompanied by their musical and dancing choirs. Whenever a visiting fellowship arrives, multitudes of the laity accompany them, vying with them in zeal and enthusiasm. The mystics visit various neighboring shrines in the area, on their way to the shrine of the celebrated Wali.

The visiting fellowships—just like the local fellowships—perform *zikr* [see page 62 and Appendix C] sessions throughout the duration of the octave-week festival, to heighten their spiritual experiences, with the spiritual presence of the Wali. The *zikr* takes place throughout the afternoon and evening at the *mouleds*, usually in special tents, but can be in public places and in houses also.

In addition to the performance of *zikrs* and the visits to the shrine, all mystical (Sufi) fellowship members participate in all other activities in the *mouled*—entertainment, sports, boy circumcision, dispensing protective charms, etc. They provide an excellent role model for the young and the old who attend the *mouled*. They lead by example, and as a result the crowds are attracted to them and in most cases, many new members are recruited at the *mouleds*.

3. Visitation Obligations

The central religious act at a *mouled* is the visit to the shrine by the public (men, women, children of all ages and classes), in honor of the **Pir/Mir/Wali**. Pilgrimage to a shrine is called a visitation, while the shrine itself is called a place of visitation. The public's visitation to the shrine during the *mouled* is an essential component of the intent of the annual festival—rejuvenation. Visitations are conducted every day of the *mouled's* duration (8 days), usually in the afternoons.

There is a certain etiquette for visitation. The person must be clean and enter the room by greeting the **Wali**, and asking permission of the **Wali** to enter or leave. People circle the shrine several times—usually seven, with ejaculations eulogistic of the **Wali**. They dispense incense and talk to the **Wali** loudly, quietly, or in silence. Small earthenware lamps and/or candles are lit and placed in the shrines. Flowers are also offered. When leaving, the visitor must ask permission from the **Wali** to leave, and must say the proper farewells.

People visit the celebrated **Wali** for basically three reasons:

A. As an obligation and a duty. [See chapter 7.]

B. To receive **Ba-ra-ka** of the **Wali** by visiting the shrine and monument within (*maksoorah*). To receive the **Wali's Ba-ra-ka**, visitors place their hands first on the *maksoorah* and then on the face. Women use scarves to rub the monument and take them home to rub other people in their villages who could not attend the *mouled*.

C. To obtain special favors from the **Pir/Mir/Wali**, such as curing illness, getting pregnant, etc. For this purpose, one must make a vow with the **Wali** [more details to follow].

4. Feast of Offerings

The offerings presented during the *mouled* constitute a major component of the festival [see significance of offerings in chapter 7]. On behalf of the celebrated Wali, food and drinks are made available to the visitors of the *mouled* in two ways:

a - via offerings specified by the Pir/Mir/Wali, and sponsored by his lineage mystical keepers.

The Pir/Wali, who specifies the location(s) of his shrine(s) and the visitation schedule, also specifies the types and amounts of offerings that will be distributed to the needy at his/her annual festivities.

Representations of Egyptian men and women loaded with provisions going in procession to the shrines of their deceased are very common in tomb-chapels, more than 5000 years ago [as shown herein from the tomb-chapel of Ty]. The same thing still occurs in Egypt. *Baladi* Egyptians believe that  it is our responsibility to maintain a vital relationship with the Walis at their shrines, by providing such offerings.

b - via individuals as a result of special vows.

A person who seeks Ka-ra-ma-at (special favors, but not of a selfish nature such as becoming a millionaire, etc) from the Wali, must make a vow that, if he recovers from a sickness, or obtains a son, etc, he will donate certain thing(s) to the public, on the Wali's behalf. The moral contract with the

Wali (in the form of a vow), is fulfilled by donating to the public and not to any religious authority. If the vower attains his object/request, he fulfills his promise. For example, he might sacrifice an animal and make a feast with its meat for any persons who visit the shrine. Having given the animal to the Pir/Mir/Wali, he thus credits the latter with feeding the poor. Ancient and *Baladi* Egyptians ate/eat the meat of the sacrificed animals, so as to be blessed by the Wali him/herself.

As a result of offerings and fulfillment of vows, abundant food and refreshments are available to all, provided by the holy host (Wali), courtesy of anonymous givers.

5. Boy Circumcision (Initiation)

The Egyptian *mouleds* provide a blessed time to perform boy circumcision, especially during the *Tear Drop Mouled*. [See pages 92-3.]

Boy circumcision symbolizes a new *birth* for the boy who is being transformed (died and reborn as a man), which is consistent with the renewal theme of the *mouled*.

The initiation process of the boy to manhood can be a private ceremony, with the operation at home, or a public ceremony. Most people choose a public initiation process where the boy candidates are paraded through the streets with their friends in open carriages. The small procession is usually augmented by a brass band.

Circumcision tents/booths are found in the *mouleds*. The operation is conducted by mystical (Sufi) members of the artisan fellowships, and are generally free of charge.

6. Variety Booths

Kiosks and booths are spread around the district of the shrine to sell a variety of food, refreshments, cotton candy, sugar figurines, beer, souvenirs, etc. There are also kiosks, manned by mystics (Sufis), to dispense protective charms, foretell destinies—by cards (Tarot) and other means.

One of the unique features of the Egyptian *mouled* is the sugar figurine—lovingly shaped and called *The Bride of the Mouled*. This is consistent with the essence of inner marriage that permeates all types of activities and practices of the Egyptian model of mysticism.

7. The Mystical Entertainment

As stated earlier, social and entertainment activities can't be separated from the purely religious aspects of the *mouled*. In addition to entertainment, these activities assist in teaching, rejuvenating, reinforcing cultural values, as well as preserving societal traditions.

Entertainment options are found everywhere in the spirited fairs. There is always a variety of entertainment programs—animated poetry recitations, storytelling, singing, dancing, stage plays, etc. These programs take place in a variety of theaters, such as: a platform outside a cafe, shop, or house; a screen of canvas or a tent; a passage between the buildings; or a huge tent with bleachers surrounding an arena big enough for a circus.

The performers include storytellers, actors, singers, musicians, dancers, clowns, dwarfs, giants, muscle-dancers, mimes, etc. All activities are engaging, with the public of all

ages and classes participating in singing, clapping, dancing, etc. All the attendants are absorbed and intoxicated
by the animated activities.

All these types of entertainment
are regularly used in the *mouleds* to
convey knowledge and wisdom. By ex-
aggerating (dramatizing) the behavior
of the characters of the story, people
can see themselves in these characters and learn to improve
their own behavior. All the different modes of entertainment
emphasize virtues and good behavior, benefits of marriage,
family values, work ethics, accountability, etc.

8. The Mystics' Sports and Games

Games play a major role in the *mouled* where people can
watch some events and participate in others.

Ancient and classical writers affirmed that games owe
their development, if not their very origin, to religious observances. Many accounts of games are mentioned by Homer
as essential to the accompaniment of devotional ceremonies.

Long ago, before the Greeks and Romans, games were
(and continue to be) performed in honor of certain **neteru**
(gods). Such games included (but were not limited to) wrestling and other gymnastic exercises. Diodorus, in *Book I* (16),
affirms such a role:

> *It was by Tehuti (Hermes), for instance, according to the Egyp-
> tians, that . . . . he was the first . . . .* **to establish a wrestling
> school, and to give thought to the rhythmical movement
> of the human body and its proper development.** *. . . .*

Here we find again that **Tehuti's** domain extends to the maintenance of a healthy body through rhythmic movements and sports.

The Egyptian mystics (Sufis) are physically and mentally fit. They display their talents in the *mouleds*. A sample of games performed by the Egyptian mystics (Sufis) in the *mouleds*, which one can watch include:

- The ritualistic, graceful wooden sword play and dances, performed to musical tones of the Egyptian double pipe known as the *mizmar*.
  The game requires tremendous agility, strength, and concentration.

- Display of horsemanship by making horses dance or prance, or paw the ground. Also, the Egyptian mystics (Sufis) participate in a variety of games while on horseback, diverse horse races, etc.

- Wrestling games that constitute a perfect combination of ritual and sportsmanship. Wrestling is mentioned in the holiest of Ancient Egyptian texts, and was considered an important element of the most religious activities of the Ancient Egyptian festival (*mouled*).

- Displays of extra-human strength/skills (at no charge), which some may call magic—such as performances of mastery over pain by eating fire, glass, live snakes, etc.

- Acrobatic and balancing acts, like in a circus.

For light entertainment, the public can participate and enjoy games testing their strength, coordination, and concentration. Some unique examples are:

- Crack shots with small rifles at a tiny target.
- Throwing a ball at nine pins (bowling).
- Ringing the bell at the top of a pole with a hefty swing of a mallet onto an anvil.

All other games of luck, and fun rides such as the ferris wheel, carousel, etc., which can be found in fairs throughout the world, are also found in the Egyptian *mouled*.

9. The Climactic Octave Eve Activities

The last night (which is the 8th) of the *mouled* is a very special evening. Increased activities take place starting around mid-afternoon, including several processions to the shrine of the venerated Wali and other shrines in the district, as well as *zikr* performances from the various visiting mystical (Sufi) fellowships.

Ancient Egyptian tomb-chapels show festive banquets with elaborate preparations that have been brought to the area for the celebration, including: carpets, chairs, tables, food, beverages, flowers and ointments.

These festive banquets continue to be held at the end of prominent *mouleds*, where a great reception is offered/provided for the visiting fellowship members, so they can meet each other in a happy atmosphere.

The public becomes very involved in all types of activities on this very special evening, to the early hours of the morning of the last day of the *mouled*. The happiness and joy of the crowds is indescribable.

10. The Closing Cermonies—The Final Procession

The ultimate "seal" of the festivities follows the *Great Eve*. It involves the circling of the shrine at noon by the mystic (Sufi) fellowships, to pay their final respects. In some *mouleds*, the *Great Zaffa (Procession)* is combined with the final shrine rituals on this last day. These last rites take place during the pulling down of decorations, variety booths, stage theaters, etc.

Most final processions begin in the mid-afternoon at a major square. All visiting mystic (Sufi) fellowships join in the *Great Zaffa (Procession)*, each with their distinguishable banners, robes, staves, etc. They walk in their special way that borders on dancing with much zeal and enthusiasm. Some members of the participating fellowships play musical instruments and perform ritualistic dances.

The *Great Zaffa* also includes one or more ferry boats, borne on shoulders of men or mounted on animals. A small model of a boat is usually hung up in the shrines of many Walis, the boat being called the Wali ferryboat. The boat, with a sort of canopy, is placed on its frame prior to the beginning the procession, and holds an effigy or sacred object related to the venerated Wali.

Likewise in Ancient Egypt, several divine arks (boats) participated in the processions. The ark stood on a pedestal in the Holy of Holies in the temple or the various shrines, and was drawn in procession by the priests on festive occasions.

The divine ark (boat), was often called wts nfrw, *"the one who raises on high the beauty (of the neter/Wali)"*. The sacred ark (boat) in Egyptian traditions symbolizes the power of self-renewal. The boat is qualified as a *"divine being and savior from the death"*.

An example of a typical Egyptian ferry boat is depicted herein. Note the presence of the **Ba**, representing the soul of the **Wali**, on top of the canopy, which contains an embodiment of the **Wali's Ka**, such as an effigy or a relic.

The procession of the sacred arks (ferry boats) is frequently depicted in sculptures throughout Egypt, such as in the case of the **Apet** Feast, which celebrated the one mile (2 km) journey of **Amen/Amun/Amon** from his sanctuary at Karnak Temple to the temple of Luxor and back again. The statue of **Amen** traveled partly on land, carried in a model boat on the shoulders of the priests, and partly in a real boat on the River Nile, while crowds of spectators gathered along the banks. Scenes from an **Apet** Feast, celebrated during the reign of Tutankhamen, decorate the walls of a colonnade in the Luxor temple, and give a lively impression of the occasion.

The present-day Egyptians of Luxor perform the same ancient festivities, starting at the Abu-el-Haggag mosque, located at Luxor Temple, and following the same ancient traditions camouflaged in an Islamic exterior. It is a testament to the resiliance of the *Baladi* mystical Egyptians.

The *Great Zaffa (Procession)* also includes

acrobats, jugglers, wrestlers, singers, dancers, musicians, etc.

At the end of the procession, the climax of the *Great Zaffa* is the appearance of the Wali's successor (a spiritual or blood descendant) or his representative, riding a horse (symbol of nobility) or a donkey (symbol of humility).

The crowds line up in the streets and fill the balconies along the route of the procession, shouting, waving, singing, clapping, dancing, laughing in an ecstatic atmosphere.

It is an atmosphere of absolute ecstasy and the Pir/Mir/Wali would have not wanted it any other way.

Part

||||

Come One Come All

11

Fellowship Formations

The Universality of Egyptian Mysticism

Throughout this book, it has been shown that the Egyptian model of mysticism (now known as *Sufism*) is not attached to (or an offshoot of) Islam. The natural principles and practices of the Egyptian model are as common in the West as in the East. A mystical seeker is anyone who believes that it is possible to have direct experience of God. The Egyptian model of mysticism is a natural expression of personal religion. The seeker has the right to pursue a life of contemplation, seeking contact with the source of being and reality. The mystical seekers pursue knowledge of the Reality/Truth of God that cannot be gained through dogmatic religions.

Technically speaking, one does not have to be a born/converted Moslem to adopt and practice this model of mysticism. However, it is true that being a born/converted Moslem is a prerequisite to join a *"Sufi"* fellowship in a presently Islamized country. Such a requirement is caused by fear of the wrath of Islamists in these countries and nothing more. As a matter of fact, these mystical principles and practices are contrary to Islam, as explained throughout this book.

In addition to the common misconception that *"Sufism"* is an offshoot of Islam, there is a general tendency to lump very different types of mysticism (known as *"Sufism"*) into one category—erroneously labeled *Mystics of Islam.*

The Egyptian mystical (Sufi) teachings and practices are markedly different than those of Sufis in other countries, as is contrasted throughout this book.

The Countless Ways

The Egyptian model of mysticism (Sufism) is not a matter of creed and dogma, but rather of a personal charter. Each one of us is a unique individual. The Ancient Egyptians implemented their beliefs in the individuality of each of us, in all their texts. For example, there were never two identical transformational (funerary) or medical (so-called "magical") texts for any two individuals. There is no one-size-fits-all dogmatic doctrine.

The Egyptian model recognizes the uniqueness of each individual, and as such recognizes that the Paths to God are as numerous as the number of seekers. The ways to God are like the streams—they all go to one source. All Egyptian thinking is based on this principle—*variations on a theme.*

The mystical seekers generate their own kinds of collective life. Like-minded seekers form networks of masters and disciples called the *Ways.* The framework of a *Way* is better described as a fellowship. An Egyptian model mystic fellowship (order) can be formed anytime and anywhere.

The diversity of humankind is reflected in the diversity of fellowships. Hence, fellowships vary in their nature, teachings, exersises, etc. The diverse nature of organized fellowships follow—in general terms—the nature of the four elements of the universe, namely: fire, air, earth, and water.

The Principles of a Fellowship

All fellowships must contain the following elements:

1. A link to a spiritual chain.
2. A systematic organization consisting of members at various stages of development/progression.
3. A code of ethics.
4. Modes and programs to attain fellowship goals.
5. An active role in society.

1. A Link to a Spiritual Chain

In order for the aspirants of a fellowship to gain knowledge through spiritual revelation, one or more members of the fellowship must be a spiritual medium who can communicate and connect, through the chain of past spiritual guides, to a **Pir/Mir/Wali**—who is commonly known as the "founder of the fellowship". The **Pir** is the one who has achieved unification with the Divine [as explained in pages 64-5]. [The significant role of the spiritual chain, in gaining gnosis, will be detailed in Appendix C.]

Fellowships are therefore organized into spiritual lineages descending from a **Pir**, forming a mystical or devotional *Way*. The founder guarantees the availability of his **Ba-ra-ka**—a state of blessedness implying an inner spiritual power—to the members of the fellowship. Previous heads of the fellowship are known as the *Chain of Blessing* (*silsilat al baraka*). The chain of spiritual ancestry unites them with the founder of the fellowship. This chain provides accessibility to the **Pir**— the power in the sky.

Because of the importance of the spiritual chain, each

mystical (Sufi) fellowship is referred to as a *silsila*—a chain. Each fellowship contains an unbroken chain of well trained guides. The chain began with the **Pir**—the founder, who selected the most spiritually gifted among his group to be his successor. Later on, this successor chose the most spiritually gifted as his successor (like the **Pir** did), and so on.

It is always better, but not necessary, for the fellowship members to meet in a place close to one of the original founder's shrines, or any of the subsequent heads of the fellowship, as *a place of contemplation.* In any event, a relic of the **Pir** should always be available at their meeting place.

Membership in a mystical fellowship is obtained by binding oneself by oath to the head or guide of a fellowship or, if the two do not coincide, to a spiritual master who is himself attached to the spiritual chain of **Ba-ra-ka**, and who is the spiritual leader/guide of the fellowship at the present time.

The present spiritual leader/guide need not be perfect or all-knowing. What is important is that he is capable of connecting to the previous leader who in turn connects to his prior guide, etc. The chain is like a pipeline, in which each spiritual guide is a section of pipe. The blessings that come to each seeker flow through the pipeline. They flow through the guide, but they are not from him—the blessings are from the **Pir/Mir/Wali**. The section of pipe, for which the present leader is responsible, is tightly connected to the pipeline so that blessings can flow freely without leaking away.

Egyptian mystics (Sufis) don't like to engage in historical or geographical discussions of their groups and founders. If they do, they do so reluctantly, so Islamists will leave them alone. As a result, all fellowships (orders) in Islamized countries have to pay due lip service and "profess" that each's founder and their chain of leaders were/are devout Moslems.

2. A Systematic Organization

Each fellowship consists of like-minded aspirants who share similar natures, mindsets, outlooks, etc. These like-minded groups come from all classes: professionals, tradesmen, artisans, agriculturists, etc. In order to achieve their common objectives, it is necessary for each group to have some kind of organization.

Groups act in the form of circles of disciples working collectively around an acknowledged master of the Way, seeking training through association and companionship. They are linked to the master like soulmates.

The heart and soul of the fellowship is the person with the most spiritual power/force—**Ba-ra-ka**. His role consists of a combination of a guide/ coach/ teacher/ soulmate/ friend/ pilot/ navigator/ spiritual medium. [See more about the role of the guide in chapter 3, Appendix C, and throughout this book.]

In the West, mystical aspirants/seekers are often attracted to those who write or speak beautifully about great truths. However, in the Egyptian model, it is considered a hypocrisy to discuss the truth and not live it. Insincere teaching can weaken or even destroy a student's faith. A real mystical guide practices what he or she preaches.

The members of a fellowship are at various stages of development/progression. Those members who are more advanced act as guides/coaches for others. There is not a clear line of distinction between clergy and laity like there is in Christendom. Each member is learning, and at the same time is passing on his knowledge to a newer member.

The members of these fellowships usually take a vow of fidelity, and continue to perform their duties as citizens. The members must have productive work to support themselves and their dependants. There is no retirement from the world, i.e. no monks or hermits. The Egyptian model emphasizes a balance between living in the world and seeking spiritual experiences.

Regarding financing in the fellowship in the Egyptian model, there are no required or voluntary fees/contributions. There is no compensation to anyone in the organization. The aspirants/seekers and guides are self-supported by their jobs. Finding a place(s) to meet does not require special financing. It could be a public, private, or semi-private place.

Women are very much involved in all activities in the Egyptian mystical model, and are disciples of **Pir/Mir/Wali** and even become **Pirs/Mirs/Walis** in their own right. Some fellowships in Islamized countries circumvent the prohibition of female membership in their fellowships by establishing a women's section in a voluntary association. But other fellowships make no such organizational adjustments, and women participate outright in all activities.

Participation at all levels in the fellowship is "preferred". However, frequent absences from group activities without good reason would be considered as a lapsed membership.

These fellowships are not cults. Anyone can come and go whenever he/she wants. Though all members are free to leave a fellowship and join another, or even just leave the fellowship, it is very rare that any do.

3. A Code of Ethics

Relationships in the Egyptian model of mystical seeker (Sufi) fellowships/Ways are governed by a noble code of ethics and a standard of etiquette that are essential to traveling the spiritual path. This code is called *adab/o-sool*, meaning *discipline, pious courtesy, the right things to do*. These norms, values, and requirements are a critical part of the whole experience, which encompass practical daily piety and cultivation of gnostic and philosophic vision.

The etiquette encompasses the mystic's relationship with God, his guide, his fellow disciples, his community, and everything in the animated world around him.

Present-day traditions of *adab/o-sool* are an extension of the Ancient Egyptian **Ma-at** principles [see page 45].

4. Modes and Programs to Attain Fellowship Goals

The goals of the fellowships are to provide their members with the needed tools to achieve: self-development, character (virtue) building, companionship, good counseling, mystical training (spiritual alchemy), and inner experience informed by revelation.

Each guide/teacher provides his own program as he sees fit, to cultivate ethical and meditative goals. The teacher/guide maintains a balance between individual learning needs and the group collective learning activities. The guide is often referred to as the sun and the disciples as planets—a balance is maintained between the individual orbit of each seeker (planet) and the group (planetary/solar system) activities.

Programs in the fellowships are flexible enough to accommodate the various natures, speed, interests, etc of the aspirants. The amount of social and ritual interaction of the members, and the degree of cohesiveness and group solidarity are essential for the group success.

A guide will help the mystical aspirant organize his/her actions into progressive stages along his/her path. Both the guide and the mystical aspirant establish and agree to a projected plan. The guide explains the plan to the mystical aspirant. Both the guide and the aspirant agree on any needed revisions to the plan, and the final conclusion is contributed by both parties. The guide may cancel the agreement if the seeker does not live up to the plan and/or refuses to perform required tasks.

5. An Active Role in Society

The Egyptian model of mysticism emphasizes that the adherents must be active participants in the society. Examples of such active roles are:

A. Members must be involved in society by practicing what they learn. Serving others constitutes an integral aspect of self-development. The individual performance in the society is the true test of his/her success.

B. Shrines of the venerated **Walis/Pirs** must be maintained by the mystical seekers, so as to make them available for visitors' use. Shrines provide ritual and spiritual counsel, medical cures, and mediation among different groups and strata of the population. The shrines were/ are also significant centers for local festivals.

C. Members sponsor, organize, and participate in the rites and ceremonies—both religious and secular—of their respective fellowships, at the annual festivals of **Walis**.

D. Fellowship members are expected to make journeys to nearby communities, in order to participate in their *mouleds*.

The various fellowships set up a pattern of mutual hospitality between each other.

E.   As a source of blessings, they must provide **Ba-ra-ka** to those seeking blessings for their worldly affairs. As stated earlier, any acquired supernatural powers/talents of the mystical seekers must be made available to whoever needs them. **Ba-ra-ka** is a gift (from God) that must be returned back in the form of service to mankind and the world.

12

Auset (Isis)
The Model Philosopher

The most effective way to convey knowledge and wisdom (and for such information to reach the hearts and the minds of all people) is to organize the information into a well formed story. The Egyptian story of **Auset** (Isis) and **Ausar** (Osiris) explains practically all facets of life. Plutarch, in his *Moralia* (Vol V), provided a good overview of the Egyptian concept of **Ausar** and **Auset**, with its many facets.

At this time, we will focus on the aspects of the story that relate to the model philosopher (in its original meaning of *truth lover*)—namely **Auset** (Isis). **Ausar** (Osiris) is **Auset's** divine love, who is described in the Ancient Egyptian texts as the *Manifester of Truth*.

In the Egyptian model story, **Ausar**, the *Manifester of Truth*, was tricked by **Set** (Seth) and his accomplices into lying down inside a makeshift coffin. The evil group quickly closed and sealed the chest, and threw it into the Nile. **Ausar** died and his coffin flowed into the Mediterranean Sea.

Meanwhile, **Auset,** upon receiving the news of **Ausar's** death and disappearance, was in grief and vowed never to rest until she found the *Manifester of Truth*—**Ausar.**

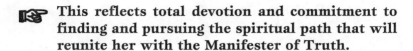 **This reflects total devotion and commitment to finding and pursuing the spiritual path that will reunite her with the Manifester of Truth.**

Auset searched everywhere, accosting everyone she met, including children, for it was said that children had/have the power of divination.

1. To search for the truth one must go near and far, accosting—never leaving a stone unturned.

2. Children represent the power of divination, which is a mode of gaining knowledge that is beyond our limited human senses.

The story goes that one day during her search, **Auset** requested shelter at the house of a poor woman.

This point signifies the paramount feature of the Egyptian model where the mystical seekers are taught not to consider themselves superior to others, but to rank themselves as the poorest, lowest, and most humble of mankind.

The story continues that the coffin of **Ausar** was taken by the waves to the shoreline of a foreign land. A tree sprang up and grew around it, enclosing the body of **Ausar** in its trunk. The tree grew large, beautiful, and fragrant. News of this magnificent tree came to the king of this alien land, who ordered that the tree be cut down, and its trunk brought to him. He utilized the trunk as a pillar in his house without knowing the great secret it contained within.

 This is reference to the Tree of Life, and with all that that implies. It is also a reference to the Tet (Djed) pillar of Ausar (Osiris).

Auset had a revelation in her dreams that Ausar's body was in this alien land, so she immediately traveled there. When she arrived she dressed as a commoner and befriended the queen's handmaidens and was able to get a job in the palace as a nurse of the baby prince.

 1. Auset (Isis) represents the purified Egyptian mystics, whose knowledge is revealed to them in dreams or in trance states.

2. Auset, the Queen of Egypt, personifies the Egyptian model of mysticism that emphasizes the practice of humility in the world. As stated earlier in chapter 4, the Egyptian mystical aspirants practice humility by serving others without exception.

Later on, Auset confessed her identity to the queen, and the purpose of her mission. Auset (Isis) then asked the king that the pillar be given to her. The king granted her request, and she cut deep into the trunk and took out the chest.

Later, Auset returned back to Egypt with the chest containing Ausar's dead body. She hid the body in the marshes of the Nile Delta. Auset used her magical powers to transform herself into a bird. Drawing Ausar's essence from him, she conceived a child—Heru (Horus). In other words, Auset was impregnated by the holy ghost of Ausar.

 1. This immaculate conception is indicative of the inner marriage that permeated Ancient Egyptian

(and Sufi) traditions. In the concept of inner marriage of the self (Ka) and the soul (Ba), Auset represents the bird (Ba), and Ausar represents the self (Ka). [See an illustration of this concept on page 115.]

2. It should also be noted that Auset's conception of Heru (Horus) by no living man is the oldest version of immaculate conception.

The story continues that one night when the moon was full, the evil Set and his accomplices found the chest containing the dead body of Ausar and cut him into 14 pieces (the 14 symbolizes the number of days required to shape a full moon). Ausar represents the lunar principle in the universe and is known as *Ausar the Moon*.

When Auset (Isis) heard about how Set and his accomplices cut Ausar into different pieces, and scattered them throughout the land, her job was to search near and far, so as to collect and put the broken pieces back together.

 1. *To bind or tie together* **is the meaning of the Latin word** *religio*, **which is the root of the word** *religion*. **The action of Auset symbolizes the Unity of Multiplicity—the goal of the mystic.**

2. By remembering and recollecting the story of Auset and Ausar, we keep in our hearts a tale that expresses, in Joseph Cambell's words, *"the immanence of divinity in the phenomenal forms of the universe."* [Also see page 138.]

3. One re-*members* and re-*collects* in order to heal and in order never to forget. The most prominent Egyptian mystical practice is called *zikr*—**meaning** *remembrance* [see Appendix C].

During her search for the broken pieces, **Auset** (Isis) sought the assistance of **Anbu** (Anubis), the divine guide, to serve as her guide and guard. She also sought the help of **Tehuti** (Thoth), who provided knowledge and wisdom in her spiritual path.

 1. This signifies the need for spiritual guidance in your journey. Anbu represents (like a dog) the (spiritual) path finder.

2. Knowledge and wisdom, as represented by Tehuti, are needed in traveling the spiritual path.

Auset, with the help of others, collected all the pieces... all except the phallus, which had been swallowed by a fish in the Nile. She then reunited the dismembered body of **Ausar** and, with the help of others, wrapped it in linen bandages, and mummified it.

Tehuti, **Auset**, and **Heru** performed the *Ceremony of Opening The Mouth* upon the mummy, and **Ausar** was brought back to life as the Judge and King of the Dead (the past), while **Heru** (Horus) was to take his place as king of the living (the present).

 This represents the everlasting perpetual cycle of the spiritual power on earth: *The King is dead (Ausar); Long live the King (Heru).*

Appendices

Miscellaneous Sufi Terms and Their Ancient Egyptian Roots

1. The Gazelle's symbolism

References to the gazelle (ghazelle) are widely used in Sufi (and Egyptian) traditions and can be found in countless poems and songs. Since Ancient Egyptian times, the gazelle (ghazelle) has been associated with the region of the beloved departed souls. The gazelle symbolism is found in Ancient Egypt at least since the time of the *Pyramid Texts* (ca. 4500 years ago), where it shows **Heru** (Horus), together with **Auset** (Isis), **Anbu** (Anubis), and **Tehuti** (Thoth), searching for **Ausar** (Osiris). The *Pyramid Texts* show that **Heru** finds his father, namely **Ausar**, in the *Land of the Ghazelles*.

In the annual Egyptian King's jubilee (the **Heb-Sed** Festival), where the King is renewed from **Ausar** to **Heru**, we find that the prow of the sacred ark, borne during the procession, ends in inward-facing gazelle's heads to symbolize the region of **Ausar** — the beloved departed souls.

It should be noted that *ghazl* (an adjective form of *ghazelle*) means to be *amorous*, which is consistent with the concept of the inner marriage, which permeates the Ancient Egyptian (and later Sufi) traditions.

2. Music of the Stones

Islamized Sufism makes reference to the music of the stones (planets). The Egyptian understanding of *universal harmony,* in an astronomical-musical sense, was confirmed by early Greek and Roman writers. Diodorus of Sicily, in his *Book I* [Section 16-1], states:

> *It was by Tehuti (Thoth), according to ancient Egyptians. . . [who] was the first to observe the orderly arrangement of the stars and the harmony of the musical sounds and their nature.*

The natural tones of the seven planets (closest to us on earth) provided the archetype for both the Ancient Egyptian music and the days of the week.

The Roman writer, Dio Cassius, explained how the Egyptians related the seven musical notes to the seven planets [shown herein] and the seven days of the week. [Also see page 78.]

Sufi traditions consider Tehuti's music as the means of transmission and intermediation between human and Divine, and as such it has become closely associated with the Philosophers' Stone. It is

- ♄ Saturn *[lowest pitch]*
- ♃ Jupiter
- ♂ Mars
- ☉ Sun
- ♀ Venus
- ☿ Mercury
- ☾ Moon *[highest pitch]*
- ◯ Earth

precisely the music of the stones/planets, and as such, according to Sufi traditions, the Philosophers' Stone is associated with the Egyptian **neter** (god), **Tehuti** (Thoth).

3. The Word of God

Early Islamized Sufi traditions acknowledge that the world was created through a word from **Tehuti** (Thoth)—eight characteristics (four symbolized as "gods", four as "goddesses") were made from a sound that he uttered. The same traditions state that the eightfold character of Sufi teaching is symbolized by the octagonal diagram for the word, **Hu/Hw**—the "Sufi" sound. These Islamized Sufi traditions are Ancient Egyptian concepts, as follows:

a. **Tehuti** (*Hermes*—Greek, *Mercury*—Roman) was/is called *Master of the City of Eight*. This Egyptian city was/is called **Khmunu** (*Hermopolis* by the Greeks), which means *eight*. **Tehuti's** number—eight—is the rhythmic number in the universe.

b. The eight characteristics (consisting of four pairs of **neteru/** gods/goddesses) represent the pre-creation state of matter, which in Ancient Egyptian texts is called **Nun**. The four pairs are: **Nun-Naunet, Heh-Hehet, Kek-Keket,** and **Amen-Amenet.**

c. Egyptian creation texts repeatedly stress the belief of creation by the Word. When nothing existed except the One, He created the universe with His commanding voice. The Egyptian *Book of the Coming Forth by Light* (wrongly and commonly known as the *Book of the Dead*), the oldest written text in the world, states:

> I am the Eternal ... I am that which created the Word ... I am the Word...

In Ancient Egypt, the *words* of **Ra** (Re), revealed through **Tehuti**, became the things and creatures of this world, i.e. the words (meaning sound energies) created the forms in the universe.

d. Hu/Hw [shown herein] is an Ancient Egyptian **neter** (god) representing the authoritative utterance—an aspect of the intellectual power of **Tehuti** (Thoth).

4. The Names of God

The Sufi traditions speak of the powers of the names of God. In Ancient Egyptian traditions, names are considered very powerful, as they constitute the essences of the manifested universe. We find that in the *Book of the Divine Cow* (found in the shrines of Tut-Ankh-Amen), Ra creates the heavens and its multitude, merely by pronouncing some words whose sounds alone evoke the names of things—and these things then appear at his bidding. As its name is pronounced, so the thing comes into being. For the name is a reality—the thing itself. The world and all it contains is nothing other than a manifestation of God in his attributes/names.

The role of the name in Ancient and *Baladi* Egypt was not, as per our modern-day thinking, a mere label. The name of a **neter/ netert** (god/goddess), person, animal, or principle, represents a resume or synopsis of the qualities of that person or object. The learned and most trusted people in Egypt knew/know the great real (or secret) names of the **neteru** (gods) and other cosmic forces, and used/use this knowledge very carefully.

Invocation of names of God (**neteru**) has a great impact on both the world and the human beings. Man, to the Ancient Egyptians, was the embodiment of the laws of creation. As such, the physiological functions and processes of the various parts of the body were seen as manifestations of cosmic functions. The limbs and organs had a metaphysical function, in addition to their physical purpose. As a consequence, each part of the body was consecrated to one of the **neteru** (divine principles), which appeared in the Egyptian records throughout its recovered history. This concept of the divinity of each member is summed up in the *Papyrus of Ani*, (pl. 32, item 42), as follows:

> **There is no member of mine devoid of a neter** (god)**, and Tehuti** (Thoth) **is the protection of all my flesh.**

By pronouncing the Divine Names in specific ways and in a specific order, the Cosmic Powers of the Divine will flow in an orderly fashion into the limbs and members of the mystical aspirant. [More about name calling in Appendix C.]

5. The Written Word, Sacred Geometry, etc.

Islamized Sufism writes about the art of calligraphy and the science of letters. The basic axiom of the science of letters is the interaction between letters and their relationship to numerical proportion. It should be noted that the number and order of the "Sufi alphabet"—*ABGDHWZHTYKLMN*...—does not follow the number and sequence of Arabic, Persian, or Turkish alphabets. The reason for that is that it is a purely Egyptian alphabet.

The Greek term for the Ancient Egyptian language—*hieroglyph*—means *holy script* (*hieros* = *holy, glyphein* = *impress*), indicative of the sacredness of Ancient Egyptian writings.

The Ancient Egyptians called their language **Metu Neter**, meaning *word of **neter** (god)*. Plato's *Collected Dialogues* affirms the Ancient Egyptian intent of their language, in *Philebus* (18-d):

> *...he [Tehuti] conceived of 'letter' as a kind of bond of unity, uniting as it were all these sounds into one, and so he gave utterance to the expression 'art of letters,' implying that there was one art that dealt with the sounds.*

Tehuti (Thoth) set the principle of the written language—letters—as the graphic representation (image/picture) of the spoken/sound vibrations. This point illustrates the intimate relationship between the sound and the visual (written/illustrated) forms.

The image of each Egyptian symbol (letter) contains its specific vibrational pattern. In other words, the written form manifests the unity of sound (speech) and form (script). The composition of words and phrases in Ancient Egypt followed the same rules for musical composition. The Egyptian words were constructed of their symbols (letters), so that the meaning of a word emerged from the interplay of symbols—as the meaning of a chord or a musical phrase results from the combination of notes.

[Regarding numerology, sacred geometry, and design of buildings in Ancient Egypt, see *Egyptian Harmony: The Visual Music*, by same author.]

6. The Heart and the Tongue

Heru   Tehuti

The symbolism of the heart and the tongue permeates Sufi traditions. As stated in chapter 4, such symbolism is found in the Ancient Egyptian traditions, whereby the active faculties of the Perfected Person are identified as being the heart and tongue. **Heru** (Horus), representing the heart, and **Tehuti** (Thoth), representing the tongue, are shown in numerous illustrations in the Ancient Egyptian temples and tombs, performing the symbolic rite of *Uniting the Two Lands*. We also find the Ancient Egyptian representation of the Perfected Person [see book cover], who is shown being purified by both **Heru** and **Tehuti**.

Heru represents conscience and will, and is identified with the *heart*. **Tehuti** represents deliverance and manifestation, and is identified with the *tongue*.

The combined action of **Heru** (Horus) and **Tehuti** (Thoth) governs the actions of all living organisms—large and small. Each action, voluntary or involuntary, is the result of *cause* and *effect*. As such, **Heru** (Horus) represents the *cause* and **Tehuti** (Thoth) represents the *effect*. The universal rule of *cause* and *effect*—symbolized by the functions of the *heart* and *tongue*—is found on the Egyptian Shabaka Stele (716-701 BCE), as follows:

> The Heart and the Tongue have power over all . . . the neteru (gods), all men, all cattle, all creeping things, and all that lives. The Heart thinks all that it wishes, and the Tongue delivers all that it wishes.

The above and several other Ancient Egyptian texts attest to the concept of Animism—that all things in the universe are animated (energized) by life forces, which concurs scientifically with the kinetic theory. Animism is also an essential element in Sufism. [More about Animism in *Egyptian Cosmology: The Animated Universe*, by same author.]

The combined role of the heart and the tongue is extended in all aspects of Ancient Egypt. Plutarch, in *Moralia V* (378,68G), states:

> *Of the plants in Egypt they say that the persea is especially consecrated to the goddess (Het-Heru/Hathor) because its fruit resembles **a heart** and its leaf **a tongue**.*

Plutarch's statement is affirmed by numerous Ancient Egyptian depictions [as shown herein] of **Het-Heru** (Hathor), springing from the Tree of Life to provide spiritual nourishment. The Tree of Life symbolism, found in Sufi traditions, is Ancient Egyptian.

7. The Canopus Mystical Doctrine

Sufi traditions speak of the *"Canopus Mystical Doctrine"*. Yet not too much explanation is offered for such a doctrine, outside Egypt.

Ka-Anbu (Anubis)

Canopus represents the brightest star in heaven, namely **Sabt** (Sirius), which is commonly known as the *Dog Star*. Canopus is also the name of the Ancient Egyptian seaport east of present-day Alexandria. In other words, Canopus' meanings are related to Ancient Egypt.

If we write the sound of the English word, Canopus, it sounds very much like *Ka-Anubis*. The compound term of *Ka-Anubis* means the personification (**Ka**) of *Anubis*, who is a well known Ancient Egyptian **neter** (god)—**Anbu**.

Anbu (Anubis) represents the Dog Star, and he is always shown leading the arks in their voyages toward the Divine. As such, **Anbu** represents the Divine Guide. Therefore, the *"Canopus Mystical Doctrine"* represents the guidelines for those people who seek the Divine—namely the mystics.

8. The Fountain of Youth

The Sufi traditions speak of the existence of a saintly hierarchy of **Walis**—a succession of saintly beings. Supreme among these folk saints (**Walis**) is *El Khidhr*, an allegorical personage, representing the everlasting, perpetual power on earth that is transferred from one highly spiritual leader (*kutb*) to another.

The Islamized Sufi traditions also speak of *El Khidr* as immortal, because he succeeded in drinking the water of immortality—known also as the *Fountain of Life/Youth*. *El Khidr* means *sea green*.

To appease Islam, *El Khidr* is called *Elias*—the Koranic name, which is equivalent to the biblical *Elijah*.

According to the mystical canon, there are always on earth a certain number of holy men who are admitted to intimate communion with the Deity. The one who occupies the highest position among his contemporaries is called the *kutb*, meaning *axis*, *magnetic pole*, *pivot polestar*, *chief*, or *magnetizer*.

The *kutb* represents the living image of the immortal powers of *El Khidr*, in the earthly realm. The current *kutb* is chosen by the previous *kutb*. This selection is manifested in "dreams" to the spiritual heads of the mystical (Sufi) fellowships (orders).

The *kutb* is the reputed invisible head of all the mystical (Sufi) fellowships. His duty is to oversee and to serve. Therefore, he is often seen, but not recognized as such. He always has a humble demeanor and simple dress.

Three points are to be made of these traditions:

a.   The perpetual symbolism of *El Khidr*, as manifested in the succession of *kutbs,* is similar to the Ancient Egyptian traditions of power transfer, whereby, according to the Ancient Egyptian model, **Ausar** (Osiris) died and was replaced by the new King—**Heru** (Horus). [Also see page 132.]

The everlasting perpetual power, symbolized in two poles, (**Ausar–Heru**) has been continued under the title, *kuth*.

This concept of perpetual power is eloquently illustrated in the **Ausar** Temple at **Abtu** (Abydos) [as shown below], where **Heru** is being born out of **Ausar**, after **Ausar's** death.

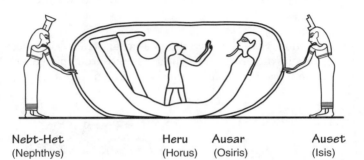

Nebt-Het	**Heru**	**Ausar**	**Auset**
(Nephthys)	(Horus)	(Osiris)	(Isis)

Accordingly, all the Pharaohs identified themselves with **Heru** (Horus) as a living King, and with the soul of **Ausar** (Osiris) as a dead King. In other words, legitimacy was balanced with two powers: the present (visible), i.e. **Heru**, and the past (invisible), i.e. **Ausar**. The right to rule was considered to be a continuous chain of legitimacy. The eternal power of the leader/King never dies. The power is merely transferred from one human body to another human body, which is translated into the common expression, *"The King is dead. Long live the King."* As if to say, *"**Ausar** is dead. Long live **Heru**."*

b. The seagreen *El Khidr* is represented in Ancient Egypt by **Ausar**, who represents the generative principle. **Ausar**, in his hawk-headed form [as shown herein], is called the *Green One* in Ancient Egyptian texts.

El Khidr is recognized by *Baladi* Egyptians as the immortal green man who appears to those who need him.

c.   The water of immortality is represented in Ancient Egypt by **Nun/Nu/Ny**, which represents the unpolarized state of matter. Every Egyptian creation text begins with the same basic concept that before the beginning of things, there was a liquidy *primeval abyss*—everywhere, endless, and without boundaries or direction. Egyptians called this cosmic ocean, **Nun**—the watery abyss, the ground state of matter from which creation arises.

As such, **Nun** is the symbolic eternal water. The successful souls in the Ancient Egyptian papyri are depicted drinking from it [as shown below]. **Nun** is sea-green in color.

It is also of great interest that the source of Islamized Sufism was from Egypt. His name was Dhu 'l-**Nun**, meaning *The Essence of Nun—The Egyptian Holy Sea*.

B

Sleeping With The Enemy
(Surviving Islam)

Theosophy was and continues to be a dangerous game to play in Islamized countries. Since the preaching of Union with God is open to the charge of blasphemy (and subsequent death), it was necessary to disguise the mystical principles and practices, to keep Islamists at bay. Islam sees itself as the final and full revelation of God. The mystics (Sufis), under the ironclad Islamic rule, have been suffering and killed by Islamists. In order to survive under the ironclad rule of Islam, the Egyptian mystics (Sufis) follow the saying, *"Stay away from Devil and sing the praises to Him"*. Here are a few examples of how these mystics continue to survive Islam:

1. Building mosques next to the shrines of the folk saints (**Walis**). In other words, they are hiding in the shadow of Islam.

2. Folk saints' shrines in the city of Tanta (in the Nile Delta) and elsewhere, contain stones that have depressions claimed to be caused by Mohammed's (who never went to Egypt) foot or palm. Mohammed's foot/palm prints guarantee the protection of these shrines. Even though Islamists don't believe such claims, they are hesitant to destroy the shrines just in case Mohammed really was there.

3. Because music, singing, and dancing are forbidden in Islam,

the mystics' (Sufi's) songs, rosaries, recitations always begin and end with praises to Mohammed and Islam. The large middle part of the rosary/recitation is related to the Wali and the spiritual lineage chain.

4.   The mystics (Sufis) were/are able to capitalize on the chaotic natures of the Koranic verses, to find ways to justify their teachings and practices. The mystics (Sufis) became more familiar with the Koran than Islamists: quoting Koranic verses out of context and finding the cracks in the Islamic doctine, and using them very well, in defense of their practices.

5.   To appease Islamists, the ecstatic practice of *zikr* begins and ends by paying homage to Mahammed, his family members, and Allah. *Zikr* is contrary to Islamic doctrine [see pages 20-21].

6.   The mystics (Sufis) use the figurative style in their expressions as a mask for mysteries that they desired to keep secret. They also use oblique meanings for common words, in order to throw off Islamists, and as a protection against accusations of heresy or civil disobedience.

7.   The mystics dress up mystical (Sufi) concepts in an Islamic garment and *generously* give the credit to Islam and Mohammed. As a result, they pay an exaggerated deference to the Islamic "Prophet" and to his cousin Ali, in order to keep on good terms with Islamists. As such, they assert (contrary to the Islamic doctrine) that Sufism had its rise in Mohammed himself, and that all the mystical (Sufi) fellowships trace their lines of succession back to him and his four successors. The mystics (Sufis) assert (contrary to the Islamic doctrine) that Mohammed has been the recipient of a two-fold revelation, the one embodied in the contents of the Koran, the other within his heart. The former was meant for all and is binding on all; the latter was to be transmitted to the chosen few through lines of succession.

8.   They state that the human being to whom God granted the most Ba-ra-ka is said to be Mohammed, who passed it to his descendants, commonly known as *shurfa*, meaning nobles.

9.   They generally identify the "Complete/Perfect Man" as Adam, but sometimes (to appease Islamists even more) they say it is Mohammed!

10. The origin of all mystical (Sufi) Ways in Egypt are claimed to come from other countries, to appease Egypt's Arab/Moslem invaders. It is therefore claimed that each major **Wali** spent time in Saudi Arabia, Iraq, Morocco, etc, in order to appease the Islamic rulers from these places.

11. Celebrating Mohammed's immediate family members' birthdays, among thousands of purely non-Islamic Ancient Egyptian festivals *(mouleds)*, is a ploy to appease Islamists.

12. All Ancient Egyptian festivals have been continued under "Islamized names".

13. Reading/reciting the Koran (usually at the beginning and very end of the *mouled*, *zikr*, etc) is a camouflage for non-Islamic activities.

14. Ancient Egyptian folkloric stories survived the Islamic rule by changing the names of characters and places. For example, a common Egyptian-told story of *The Shah of Persia and his Daughter* is almost exactly like the tale told to Herodotus about **Menkaura** (Mykerinos), his daughter, and the golden image of a cow.

15. The mystics (Sufis) use the "Islamic term" *sheikh* to refer to revered **Wali/Pir/Mir**.

16. Mystics appease Islamists by telling them that pilgrimages to the **Walis** during *mouleds* are a substitute for those who cannot make the annual Islamic pilgrimage to Mecca.

C

Zikr:
The Ecstatic Practice

Prologue

We are unaware of the existence of most of our surroundings that we do not see and hear, because their frequencies are faster/ slower than the sound and light frequencies that our senses can detect. Even though our human faculties are perceptive, they are nevertheless limited: like a radio that can only receive certain electro-magnetic waves and not other parts of this band. Our senses are most familiar with matter—the densest form of energy. Lighter and faster forms of existence are beyond our sensory capacities. The perceived world is therefore a distortion.

The goal of *traveling the Path* aims at dispersing the veils that hide the self from the Real and thereby become transformed or absorbed into undifferentiated Unity. The *zikr* practice provides the means for the purified mystical seeker to close the gap between the physical realm/nature and the metaphysical nature. *Zikr* is a particular method of approach to Reality, making use of intuitive and emotional spiritual faculties, which are generally dormant and latent unless called into play through training under guidance.

Zikr is the central ritual of the Egyptian mystics. This practice leads to the freeing of oneself from the body and the limitation of human senses. As a result, the participant's consciousness is raised, whereby the mystical seeker achieves *knowledge of God by way of revelations,* where states of visionary ecstasy exist.

Early Sufi traditions acknowledge that *zikr* was introduced into the Islamized Sufism by the Egyptian, Dhu 'l-Nun al-Misri, who said, *"zikr is absence from oneself (by recollecting God alone)."* The absence from oneself is the ideal recollection of God. The whole of Egyptian mysticism rests on the belief that when the individual self is lost, the Universal Self is found. The purified mystics strive for loss of self and absorption into the Divine, in order to obtain personal illumination and transcendence—an ecstatic visionary.

There are three terms for this practice. All three terms describe various aspects of the same practice. The following are the meanings of each term:

Zikr—means *testifying* or *remembrance*. Implicit in the term *remembrance* is the notion that we are coming back to what we once knew (through our past lives)—what we have already learned. Remembrance is achieved by each's heart and tongue [see page 140].

Hadra—means *presence*, i.e. *being in the presence of spirits in higher realms*, or *calling on higher spirits*. The response and participation of these higher spirits in the *zikr* are very important, as will be detailed later. The goal of the *zikr/hadra* is to achieve the ecstatic trance when the soul is drawn to and is absorbed for a time in the *"All-Soul"*—like a magnet.

Samaa—which in the Ancient Egyptian language means *to unite*—through sound/music. As stated earlier, Sufi traditions acknowledge that appropriate music is the means of transmission and intermediation between human and Divine. **Samaa** is the effective method/way to fulfill the desire to unite/vanish into God. In other words, the right musical compositions and sound of words/names induce a state of ecstasy.
The Egyptian Dhu 'l-Nun el-Masri said of **samaa**, *"Those who listen with their souls can hear the heavenly music/call."*

It should be noted that the concept of **samaa** is also very important in *mouleds* [see chapter 10 for more details].

What is Zikr?

Zikr is a practice performed by a group of mystical seekers, by chanting, rhythmic gestures, dancing, and deep breathing. While performing their ritualistic dance, the group repeats words and phrases accompanied by a well trained choir performing instrumental and vocal music. In *zikr*, the accompanying singing of well composed musical rosaries helps achieve the trance. The music sets the rhythm (beat), which is altered by the conductor/guide to achieve the trance conditions needed to achieve ecstatic visions.

The bodily movements of the *zikr* participants are linked to a thought and a sound or a series of sounds. The movements develop the body, the thought focuses the mind, and the sound fuses the two and orients them towards a consciousness of divine contact.

The representational sacred dance of the *zikr* is analogous to the movements of the cosmos and the oneness of the universe. The individuals performing the *zikr*—as led by their guide, are like the planets of a solar system. In other words, the guide/leader is the sun and the participant seekers are the planets—each in his own orbit—yet they are held in unison by their guide/leader.

Like the dancing planets, the mystical seekers (Sufis) participating in the *zikr* become both ritual subjects/agents, and ritual objects. They become so in the repetition of the most economical and condensed of symbols—the word. As explained in items 3 and 4 of Appendix A, it is not only the word of Divinity, but the *logos*, the word that in a mysterious sense is Divinity. [More details to follow later.]

Who Does it?

This mystical exercise is only valuable to the seekers who have:

1.   Completed the first stage of purification—both outer and inner [see chapter 4].

2. Sharpened their powers and abilities by making advancement in basic practices [see chapter 5].

3. Joined and incorporated themselves into a mystical fellowship where they found and bonded with a spiritual guide.

4. Learned, comprehended, and practiced the fundamentals of the spiritual Path.

Men may participate alone; but women may join in. Women sometimes prefer to have their own performance. The musicians and singers in *zikr* can be either men or women.

Where is it done?

Zikr may be performed privately, publicly, or semi-privately. It can be performed inside or outside a building. The most preferred place is near the shrine of the Pir/Mir/Wali. A personal relic of the Wali is always present where the *zikr* is performed.

The place where the *zikr* is held must be clean and purified by libation and the burning of incense, prior to the performance of *zikr*.

When is it Done?

Zikr is usually practiced once or twice a week, on specific days of the week, usually on Friday Eve. Thursday night is the night that is especially sacred to the Egyptian *Baladi* and their mystics, to visit the shrines and to practice religious rites.

Zikr performances by the various mystical (Sufi) fellowships are an essential ritual during the *mouleds* [see pages 106 and 113].

How is it done?

Pre-Zikr Preparation

Before performing group *zikr*, the participant seekers must prepare for it. Such preparation is misunderstood by some writers as "individual/solitary *zikr*". The preparatory work prior to *zikr* performance is basically as follows:

1.   The mystical seeker must be clean (bathed, shaved, etc), and wearing clean clothes.

2.   The mystical seeker must perform the inner purification rituals by the recitation, either aloud or in a whisper, of certain litanies as prescribed by the leader of the *zikr*. The process includes the spiritual ingestion of established formulas, sometimes with the slow swaying of the body or inclination of the head in rhythmic cadence until the requisite number—as determined by the group guide—has been completed.

3.   The mystical seeker must then concentrate all his bodily senses, expel all preoccupations and wayward impulses of the heart, and concentrate by any means. A common mode of concentration is to close the eyes, keep the lips tightly sealed, and press the tongue against the roof of one's mouth.

4.   The participant seeker must then increase his focus to prepare for an out-of-body experience by entering a dark, isolated place and/or blindfolding one's eyes. Some mystical seekers lay down in a makeshift coffin and imagine that his/her soul hovers over his/her body.

5.   While concentrating as mentioned above, the mystical seeker next performs an exercise commonly known as the "guide exercise," where the seeker concentrates intensely on the guide/ leader, keeping his image in mind even though he is absent from the room. The seeker who has established a special bond with his guide, allows himself to pass away (be absorbed) into the guide. In other words, the mystical seeker forgets his existence (his I-ness) and melts/vanishes into his guide.

The Spiritual Guide and the Heavenly Ladder

Performing *zikr* causes the participants to enter frontiers that are beyond our normal earthly existence. It is therefore that each *zikr* practice must be controlled completely by an experienced leader and his assistants. As the master of ceremony, the leader guides the *zikr* and gives instructions by gestures, clapping, a word, a phrase, etc., in order to achieve full vocal and dance coordination between the members of the group performing the *zikr*, as well as the supporting choir of singers and musicians.

The leader of the *zikr* is selected for his humility and spirituality. He must be full of concentration and self-examination. He should be moderate and not let the *zikr* go overly long, nor let it be so short that the heart is not awakened, for the goal of group *zikr* is the awakening of the heart. If it appears that the *zikr* has overexcited some or most of the participants, he changes the rhythm. He must watch that the assembly remains orderly, all saying the same thing, using the same voice and movement.

The paramount function of the *zikr* leader is his role as a spiritual medium to empower each participant seeker with the divine tools, to allow each of them to reach higher in order to gain gnosis for themselves. He provides each of the *zikr* participants the opportunity to climb to higher realms—a heavenly ladder, so to speak—in order for them to gain knowledge beyond the limitations of their human senses. The leader of the *zikr*, in his person, represents, through the chain of blessing (the *silsila* of **Ba-ra-ka**), the continuation of the mystic (Sufi) fellowship through time. He contains the past, and is the promise of the future. He is the conduit to whom grace has passed, through the spiritual chain, and from whom it will pass to his successors.

The main goal of spiritual advancement in the Egyptian model is achieved in a communalistic fashion—through the spirits of the spiritual guide/leader, the lineage chain, the founder (**Wali**), and each other. By virtue of his powers, the guide/leader becomes an active magnetic pole/focal point, connecting and activating each mystical seeker into his orbit of influence, so as to allow the spirits of the mystical seekers to connect to the chain of **Ba-ra-ka**.

A fair summary of the process, through which a mystic attains visionary ecstacy with the help of the leader of the *zikr*, is:

1. The seeker loses himself into the leader/guide and the leader receives him into himself. The seeker must become mentally absorbed in the guide/leader through a constant meditation and contemplation of him. This is carried to such a degree that he sees the guide in all men and in all things. The guide assists mentally so that the aspirant's spirit becomes bound to his own.

2. Next, the combined spirit of the *zikr* leader and the mystical aspirants loses its united spirit into the spirit of the last departed guide of the fellowship. This is made possible because the present leader had established a spiritual bond with the last deceased guide, while he was alive. It is therefore possible for the present leader to concentrate on his prior guide. A successful rendezvous will allow the melting down (self-annihilation) of the seeker-guide combined spirit into the previous guide—and thus allows each mystical seeker the opportunity to gain gnosis at that level.

    The seeker (being absorbed into the present guide) is led, through the spiritual aid of the last deceased guide, up through the chain of the departed successive leaders of the spiritual lineage of each fellowship.

3. If the seeker succeeds in reaching, learning, and comprehending on a certain level, his success will lead him to a higher realm, where he has the opportunity to learn even more.

4. Eventually, the seeker is helped to pass over to the spiritual influence of the long-deceased **Pir** or original founder of the fellowship, and he sees the latter only by the spiritual aid of the guide. If successful in gnosis attainment at that level, the seeker now becomes so much a part of the **Pir** as to possess all his spiritual powers. The mystical seeker can then reach the final stage and becomes a **Wali** himself [see page 64].

Progression of the Zikr

No two *zikrs* are ever alike. *Zikr* performances represent variations on a theme. *Zikr* may take two or more hours. In general, all *zikr* practices consist of the following major elements:

1. The formation configuration/alignments.
2. The pacing rhythms of movements.
3. Chanting and invocations of names, chain names, and words of power.

The following elaborates on the three major items that constitute a *zikr* practice:

1. Formation Configuration/Alignments

Group *zikr* formations may be in the shape of a circular or an oblong ring, or in two rows, facing each other. The preferred posture in group *zikr* is usually standing, although some groups perform their *zikr* seated.

Men and sometimes women participate in *zikr*— each is linked with the brother/sister on either side of him by clasping hands with the fingers interlaced, with the thumbs raised and pressed together, and with the hands veiled by their sleeves. The spirits of the participants affect each other and are able to communicate with each other as well as with their leader. This spiritual communication/connection is possible because the participant mystics have achieved a purified state [see chapter 4] and because the presiding leader unites the participants' actions and souls.

By holding the hand of the *zikr's* leader, each participant is able, through the leader's spirit, to enter into *zikr* in a manner more profound than usual. Nonetheless, even without physical contact, the spirits of the participants in *zikr* affect each other, through the spiritual powers of the presiding leader of the *zikr*.

2. The Pacing Rhythm of Movements

In *zikr*, there are two primary movement patterns—a revolving horizontal pattern and a vertical bowing pattern. *Zikr* begins with a slow and solemn beat, but typically the pace is quickened.

First, the participants rock back and forth. Then they sway rhythmically from side to side, nod their heads, or bend backward and forward as they chant. The presiding leader beats time by clapping his hands. Then the rhythm quickens, and they rock right and left while their feet stay on the ground. The guide/leader or his representative controls the rhythm. The speed of the chanting and the crescendo to awaken the hearts of the participants inflames their feelings, and stirs their innermost secret parts. The rhythm quickens for 10-15 minutes then it slows down.

The *zikr* is marked by a series of climaxes with soft breathing in between such climaxes, rather than a gradual building up to one particular moment which might be described as the central vital instant or section of the entire practice. These climaxes are both physical, expressed in the increasing vigor of the bodily movements and the vocal crescendo; and emotional, intensified by the other elements such as the recitation of hymns (rosaries), and the changing rhythms of music and action.

As each section of the *zikr* succeeds another section, all the actions of the members should be in consort so that there is unity of performance in every respect. The group framework for the individual (seeker) experience is associated with the emphasis on harmony and order of the group as a whole. All movements in the different stages of the *zikr* should be made in unison by all the mystical seekers in the group.

The guide and his assistants carefully control the strong possibility of hysterical behavior during the climactic moments. Their function is to regulate rather than to exhort, and to prevent the group expression from becoming completely chaotic in unpredictable individual behavior. They are agents of control, not stimulators of excitement. The assistants walk around the participant seekers correcting those who are out of rhythm and indicating by movements of the hand the right tempo for those who cannot hear the clapping of the guide or are unable to follow it. The trance-like state into which the mystical seekers move is not an unconscious state, and the individual can respond to guidance provided by the leader or his assistants. They usually do this with a gentle pressure on the arm, forcing the individual to cease performing the particular section of the *zikr* long enough for him to quieten.

Coming back down to earth

Coming back down to earth after reaching visionary ecstacy is accomplished through a gradual return to the earthly environment through managed breath control and lowering the rhythm. This process is done very carefully, so as not to cause harm to the participants—similar to the care taken when waking a sleeping person.

3. Chanting and Invocations of Names, Chain Names, and Words of Power

In Egypt, group *zikr* is often performed with the assistance of singers and musicians, to animate/"give life to" the *zikr*. While the participants in *zikr* perform their dancing movements and recite the Names of God, the singers/praisers sing the praises, eulogies, or odes (similar in nature to the Song of Solomon)—often of the eroto-spiritual type that brings joy to the heart of the participants.

The musical instruments mostly used are end-blown reed flutes (*nay*), double reed-pipes, *tri-kanun* (zithers), short-necked lutes (*oud*), *kamangas* (violins), horns, clappers, cymbols, castanets, small drums (*baz*), and tambourines.

The participant mystical seekers invoke names and words of power, while performing their ritual dance. The supporting band provides the music as well as repeating names of God, or reciting a series of rosaries (*awrad*) that are pre-determined by each individual guide and recited in special times and orders. Rosaries (*awrad*) vary in different *zikrs*, and between the different groups.

The essence of *zikr* is remembrance, i.e. connecting to the past by calling and repeating the names of God and the ancestors of the spiritual lineage of each particular fellowship. [See the significance of names in Appendix A.]

Zikr often begins with recitation of one of the Divine Names. In the Islamized Sufism, it is said that remembrance of God begins with the repetition of God's Names. This is reminiscent of the Ancient Egyptians' *Litany of Ra*—The Creator, where his 75 names are recited. [Also see page 51.]

The Invocation of the Name is the rite par excellence. One must eventually see God in all things and all things in God. The proper recitation of the Divine Names empowers the *zikr* participants with the Divine Attributes. [Also see page 138.]

In order to ensure a successful *zikr* practice, it is important to maintain unity of breath, sound (chanting), and movement. Therefore, the participants pronounce each name slowly and emphatically, with an elongation of the second syllable, throwing the head and upper body back and then forward with each recitation—maintaining the tempo and unity of movement.

The breathing pattern is intimately connected with sound patterns of Name recitation. The intimate relationship between breath and the potency of the Name gives the exercise power; it also suggests that even where words are not articulated, but reside in the inhaling or exhaling, they continue to deliver the words' power. The dominant symbol of the ritual is manifestly the Word. The Word being inherently sacred, it imparts sanctity to the ritual, rather than being sanctified by it. The most important words of invocation in *zikr* are:

a. Hu/Hw, which is a name of an Ancient Egyptian **neter** (god) representing the authoritative utterance. The word is usually pronounced during exhaling—blowing.

The proper recitations of the Name **Hu/Hw** are closely associated to the various breathing patterns during the *zikr* practice. The recitation of the Name **Hu/Hw** sometimes dissolves into a mere grunt. As a result of the physical exertion involved, the participants recite ever more quietly, until all one hears is the breathing of the participants—and the music of the singers/praisers.

b. **Madad,** which is also an Ancient Egyptian term meaning *to be recited,* and was usually placed at top of columns containing spells. The word, **madad,** is derived from the Egyptian word, **mdw/mdu,** which means *speak, talk, recite.* **Medu Neteru,** in the Ancient Egyptian language, means *(Spoken) Words of God*.

At frequent intervals during the *zikr,* **madad** is chanted by the chief hymn-singer. The ritual's primary direction during the **madad** is the mediating powers of the lineage chain operating in it, with emphasis on the latest deceased person. By invoking the names of previous guides, the present leader seeks the presence of the spiritual lineage of the fellowship (order). Therefore, the singers/praisers call out the names of the chain with intense emotion, to put the participants of the *zikr* in the hands of the spirits of the spiritual chain.

The ejaculation of the word "**madad**", as an invocation for divine aid (or strength), has a profound mystical significance with the *Baladi* population of Egypt. **Madad** is found in Egyptian poems and songs, and is used in their daily life.

The mystical seekers chant or repeat different invocations, over and over again, from one section to another, until their strength is almost exhausted. They accompany their ejaculations or chants with a motion of the head, arms, or entire body. During the whole process, they are fully conscious—like a drunk who feels nothing of himself, yet is totally aware of his surroundings.

To use the same analogy of intoxication, the participants become sober again with the help of the leader and his assistants, at the end of each *zikr* practice.

Epilogue

The participant mystical seeker reaches a certain level of consciousness every time he performs *zikr*. The experience provides him a birds-eye view of the world that is beyond the limitations of our human senses. This new enlightenment allows the mystical seeker to utilize his intellect/reason to understand/realize new aspects of the world around him/her. Gaining knowledge is a continuous process of using both faculties of intellect and intuition, to interact and enrich one another.

The unique diversity, vigor, organization, and discipline of the *zikr* performance, which is found only in Egypt, has always been noted by Westerners. The ceremony is conducted with great earnestness and solemnity.

Zikr performances are rare in some parts of India and Turkey. *Zikr* is almost nonexistent in other countries. Other Islamized Sufis talk about it, yet there is no evidence of performances. *Zikr* can only be achieved by the pure mystics [see chapter 4: The Purification Process]. Some people in other countries pretend that they have received revelations. True revelations empower the mystical seeker with supernatural capabilities. Examples of mundane evidence of such supernatural powers are: foretelling future events, reading minds (specific details such as what people did/ate, how much money is in their pockets, etc). Without evidence of gaining such supernatural powers, the revelation claim is fraudulant.

D

Reaching the Hearts and Minds (Effective Communication)

There is a human tendency to overlook, deny, or ignore one's shortcomings. In order to learn, develop, and achieve, it is easier to see oneself in his/her surroundings. To effectively communicate and influence changes in people, several forms are utilized by the mystical seekers (Sufis), such as:

1. Storytelling
2. Poetry
3. Folkloric songs and dancing
4. Proverbs
5. Humor
6. A combination of some or all the above modes.

Egyptians have an endless reservoir of such forms of teaching/knowledge. These modes become the mirror in which one sees oneself through the different actors, actions, and interactions. These modes cover every aspect of life and are easy to accept and adopt in such friendly/happy formats. All the different modes emphasize good behavior, family values, desirability and benefits of marriage, harmonic relationships, character building, societal duties, work ethics, accountability, etc.

All these modes are found in the teachings of the mystical aspirants in their various fellowships, and are also demonstrated in *mouleds*. In addition to education and entertainment, there is also the benefit of frequent and regular reinforcing/reminding of good virtues, as well as the transference of knowledge, experience, and traditions from one generation to the next.

All forms of mystical teachings have multiple meanings, depending upon how much or on what level the individual can grasp them. The 'inner dimension' of these teaching modes make them capable of revealing, according to the stage of development of the listener, more and more planes of significance.

The most distinctive characteristic of Egyptian folk literature is its poetic composition, which makes it easy to memorize. All Egyptian forms of knowledge conveyance are characterized by equlibrium, balance, and harmony between the different actions/actors. As such, it is the most successful mode of knowledge/wisdom conveyance and retention.

1. Storytelling

Stories are better than exposition for explaining the behavior of things, because the relationships of parts to each other, and to the whole, are better maintained by the mind. To convey an idea/concept/theme, the best way is to personify the factors, and dramatize the interaction between the actors in a well-designed story.

Once the inner meanings of the narratives have been revealed, they become marvels of simultaneous scientific and philosophical completeness and conciseness.

To hold the attention of the listeners, storytelling contains poetic narratives that are almost always accompanied by music. Sometimes the performers act out parts of the story. Other times, the performance includes alternation between recitation, singing, and acting, as well as involving the spectators in the different forms of the performance.

2. Poetry

Practically all Ancient (and present-day mystic) Egyptian texts are written in a poetic format. One of the chief peculiarities of Egyptian (and Sufi) poetry is that they almost always contain, concealed beneath their literal meaning, an esoteric and spiritual signification. Examples are:

a.   The ecstatics are called "*spiritual drunkards*". The drunkenness of the mystics describes the ecstatic frame of mind in which the spirit is intoxicated with the contemplation of God—just as the body is intoxicated with wine.

b.   Deep emotional love, which are allegorical representations of the yearning of the soul of man for union with the Divine, or its love of and quest for the highest type of spiritual beauty and goodness—an object attained only when the mystical seeker has successfully traveled the Spiritual Path.

3. Folkloric Songs and Dancing

Folkloric songs and dances are part of the culture and they serve both for education as well as entertainment of the masses. The rich variety of Egyptian songs, poetry, and rosaries cover all types of subjects: odes (ghazels), social issues, family values, traditions, relationships, work ethics, wisdom, spirituality, etc.

4. Proverbs

Proverbs are a type of literature that is distinguished/characterized by concise expression, clear meaning(s), an effective comparison (contrast), humor (as most of them are) and good writing. Each proverb has obvious and deep meanings. Take for example the saying, "*What goes up must come down*".

5. Humor

The Egyptian mystics are happy people. Their traditions include endless funny stories, usually on and about ourselves. For many of us, laughing at our faults is the first step in being able to recognize and confront them. Egyptians are known for their humor, as documented in their Ancient Egyptian literature, and as acknowledged by all their neighbors. Herodotus described the Egyptians as the happiest people of all the nations in the world.

One of the great bonuses in learning through humor is that even as you have a good time and doubt that you have learned anything, the lessons penetrate subtly, and stay with you, to come alive when the need arises.

Humor is incorporated into stories, proverbs, poems, songs, etc, but it can also be presented as purely humorous monologues, jokes, comical stories, etc.

E

The Egyptian vs. The Latin Calendar

The Ancient Egyptian calendar followed the Sothic year. This fact is clearly acknowledged in the Webster dictionary which defines the **Sothic year** as:

- *"of having to do with Sirius, the Dog Star"*
- *"Designating or of an ancient Egyptian cycle or period of time based on fixed year"*

The Ancient Egyptians knew that the year was slightly over 365 ¼ days. The earth takes 365.25636 days to complete one revolution around the sun.

It should be noted that the chronology of 3,000 years of Ancient Egyptian history, by modern Egyptologists, was made possible only because the Ancient Egyptians followed the Sothic Year of slightly over 365 ¼ days, i.e. 365.25636 days.

The Ancient Egyptians were able to construct a monument with perfect precision, to match their perfect calendrical calculations. At the Abu Simbel Temple of Ramses II, is a statue of Ramses II, located among other statues at the back of its sanctuary, 180ft (55m) away from the only opening to the temple. The rays of the sun have illuminated his statue, next to **Amen-Ra's** statue, on 22 February of each year for more than 3,200 years.

The difference between 365.25 days and 365.25636 days, over a span of 3200 years, is 20 days. If such a minute difference of 0.00636 days per year was not accounted for, the date of illumination of the statue would have changed from its original date many years ago. The long duration of the shrine illumination is only possible because of the accuracy of the Ancient Egyptian Sothic calendar that followed the heliacal rising of **Sabt** (Sirius)—the Dog Star.

The practical Ancient Egyptians used a calendar consisting of 12 months, each equal to 30 days. [See the Egyptian months, grouped into the Ancient Egyptian's three seasons, on next page.]

The adjustments needed to make a complete year, i.e. the difference between 365.25636 days and the 360 (30 x 12) days, were made as follows:

1. The difference of 5.25 days comes at the end of the Egyptian year, by adding 5 days every year and an additional day every 4 years. The Ancient Egyptian Year currently begins (in 2003) on 11 September. The 5/6 extra days begin on 6 September.

2. The difference of 0.00636 day (365.25636 − 365¼ days) for each year requires adding another day every (1/0.00636) 157¼ years, which the Egyptians continued to do until our present times. This is accomplished by adding an extra day every 157, 314, 471, and 629 year cycles.

When Julius Caesar came to Egypt in 48 BCE, he commissioned the astronomer Sosigenes (from Alexandria) to introduce a calendar into the Roman Empire. This resulted in the Julian calendar of 365 days a year and 366 days every leap year. The Roman (Julian) calendar was literally tailored to be fit for a King. The first day of the year was the coronation day for the Egyptian King at the end of the annual rejuvenation Jubilee—the **Heb-Sed** Festivals [see pages 85-89].

However, because the Julian calendar did not take into account that the year is a bit longer than 365¼ days, the Gregorian calendar was introduced in 1582 CE to correct this error. The Gregorian calendar is still off by about one full day every 3,000 years.

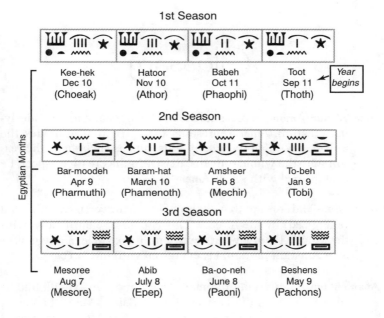

1st Season

Kee-hek	Hatoor	Babeh	Toot
Dec 10	Nov 10	Oct 11	Sep 11
(Choeak)	(Athor)	(Phaophi)	(Thoth)

Year begins

2nd Season

Bar-moodeh	Baram-hat	Amsheer	To-beh
Apr 9	March 10	Feb 8	Jan 9
(Pharmuthi)	(Phamenoth)	(Mechir)	(Tobi)

3rd Season

Mesoree	Abib	Ba-oo-neh	Beshens
Aug 7	July 8	June 8	May 9
(Mesore)	(Epep)	(Paoni)	(Pachons)

Egyptian Months

In their attempts to have a different looking calendar than the Egyptian system, both the Julian and the Gregorian calendars fell short of the exact system, as developed by the Egyptians.

The difference between 365.25 days and 365.25636 days, from the time of the adoption of the Julian calendar to our present time, is 13 days. Such a difference explains the 13 day variation in the annual observations of numerous Christian festivals—between the Orthodox and non-Orthodox churches. The reason is that one group followed the accurate Egyptian calendar, while the other group followed the inaccurate Julian calendar.

Glossary

Amen/Amun/Amon – represents the hidden or occult force underlying creation. **Amen** represents the spirit that animates the universe with all its constituents, and as such, he is the reason why the whole universe exists. In the creative aspect, he is identified with **Ra**, as **Amen-Ra**.

Animism – The concept that all things in the universe are animated (energized) by life forces. This concurs, scientifically, with the kinetic theory, where each minute particle of any matter is in constant motion, i.e. energized with life forces.

Atam/Atum – represents the manifestation of God's will, and as such represents the Perfect Human Being (Man). Likewise, Adam was/is considered to be the Perfect Man in Islamized Sufi traditions. The biblical Adam is equivalent, in some sense, to **Atam/Atum**. [Also see page 31.]

attributes – the Divine qualities and meanings that are the real causative factors of the manifested creations.

awrad – see rosary.

Baladi – see page 11, item #4.

Ba-ra-ka – a transferable quality of personal blessedness and spiritual force (almost a physical force). Also see **Ka-ra-ma-at**, which is the manifestation of **Ba-ra-ka**.

BCE – Before Common Era. Also noted in other references as BC.

Book of Coming Forth By Light (**Per-em-hru**) – consists of over 100 chapters of varying lengths, which are closely related to the *Unas Transformational/Funerary* (so-called *Pyramid*) *Texts* at

Sakkara. This book is only found, in its complete form, on papyrus scrolls that were wrapped in the mummy swathings of the deceased and buried with him.

Book of the Dead – see *Book of Coming Forth By Light*.

CE – **C**ommon **E**ra. Also noted in other references as AD.

cosmology – The study of the origin, creation, structure, and orderly operation of the universe, as a whole and of its related parts.

dhikr – see *zikr*.

El Khidr – an allegorical personage, representing the perpetual power on earth that is transferred from one spiritual being to another being. El Khidr means *seagreen*. Also see *kutb*.

fana – the state of having melted into the Divine Essence, which is followed by or alternates with *baqa* (the state of resurrecting through the Divine Essence).

hadra – see *zikr*.

Heb-Sed – Ancient Egyptian festival associated with the rejuvenation of the spiritual and physical powers of the Pharaoh.

Heka (Hike) – represents specific aspects of the intellectual powers of **Tehuti** (Thoth). **Heka** represents the ability to transform by using the right words. Therefore, **Heka** is identified with both **Sia** and **Hu**. [See pages 104-5 for more information.]

Hu/Hw – represents the authoritative utterance. **Hu** is complemented by **Sia** (consciousness). Both represent specific aspects of the intellectual powers of **Tehuti** (Thoth).

Islamized – states the actual conditions of people described as *Moslems*. *Moslem* is indicative of a free will to practice Islam. However, since Islam was forced on people many centuries ago, and because present-day born-Moslems are subject to execution by any Moslem (according to the Koran) if they renounce their religion, it is therefore more appropriate to call these hapless people *Islamized* and not *Moslems*.

Ka-ra-ma-at – represents the manifestation of the spiritual power of **Ba-ra-ka** that allows the **Pir/Mir/Wali** to perform miraculous acts, exemplary human insight, and influence/predict future events. Also see **Ba-ra-ka**.

kutb – The *kutb* represents the living image of the immortal powers of *El Khidr* on earth. He is the head of the mystical (Sufi) fellowships in a region/country. [Also see pages 65, 142-3.]

Ma-at – **netert** (goddess) of truth, right, and orderly conduct. **Ma-at** represents harmony, equilibrium, and balance. The concept of **Ma-at** has permeated all Egyptian writings, from the earliest times and throughout Egyptian history. She is the concept by which not only men, but also the **neteru** (gods/goddesses) themselves are governed. **Ma-at** is represented as a woman with an ostrich feather on her head. [Also see page 45.]

madad – an Ancient Egyptian term meaning *to be recited*, and was usually placed at top of columns containing spells. **Madad** is an invocation for divine aid (or strength) in order to unite with the spiritual lineage of the mystical (Sufi) fellowship (order).

Mir – an Ancient Egyptian term that means both *sea* and *love*. The successful mystic who attains unification with the Divine becomes the **Mir**—the *Beloved Holy Sea*. Also see **Pir** and **Wali**.

mouled/moulid – The annual renewal celebration of a **Wali** (folk saint) in Ancient and *Baladi* Egypt. Also see **Wali**.

mysticism – consists of ideas and practices that lead to *union with the Divine*. Union is described more accurately as *togetherness, joining, arriving, conjunction*, and the *realization of God's uniqueness*.

neter/netert – a divine principle/function/attribute of the One Great God. Incorrectly translated as *god/goddess*.

papyrus – could mean either: 1) A plant that is used to make a writing surface. 2) *Paper*, as a writing medium. 3) The text written on it, such as *"Leiden Papyrus"*.

Perfect Human Being (Man) – is considered to be Atam/Atum/Adam in the Ancient Egyptian as well as Sufi traditions.

Perfected Human Being – someone who has become transparent to God, and thus can reflect the Divine attributes appropriately. [See chapter 3 and pages 64-5.]

Pir – an Ancient Egyptian term meaning *shrine/spiritual embodiment*. The term is given to the mystics who are able to attain union with the Divine Essence. Also see Mir and Wali.

Pyramid Texts – a collection of transformational (funerary) literature that was found in the tombs of the 5th and 6th Dynasties (2465-2150 BCE).

Ra – represents the primeval, cosmic, creative force. His hidden name is Amen, which means *secret*. All neteru (gods) who took part in the creation process are aspects of Ra. Therefore, Ra is often linked with other neteru, such as Atum-Ra, Ra-Harakhte, etc.

remembering, remembrance (zikr) – see *zikr*.

rosary (ward/awrad/wird) – is usually a well-composed series of recitations, in the form of poetic stanzas, that are sung at specific times and on specific occasions.

samaa – an Ancient Egyptian term meaning *to unite* (through music), and as such is indicative of the means of transmission and intermediation between the human and Divine. Mostly used during *zikr* (to connect to the past leaders of the spiritual lineage) and in *mouleds* (to achieve inner marriage between the Ba and Ka of the Wali).

shaikh/sheikh – see *guide* throughout the book.

Shiite – a sect of Islam, most common in Iran and southern Iraq.

Sia – a **neter** (god) who represents the mind, consciousness, knowledge, understanding, perception, etc. **Sia** is complemented by **Hu** (authoritative utterance). Both represent specific aspects of the intellectual powers of **Tehuti** (Thoth).

silsila – see *spiritual chain*.

Sothic Year – a fixed year, having to do with **Sabt** (Sirius), the Dog Star.

spiritual chain – is a spiritual lineage descended from a **Pir** and consists of previous fellowship leaders/guides.

stanza – a group of lines of verse forming one of the divisions of a poem or song. It typically has a regular pattern in the number of lines and the arrangement of meter and rhyme.

stele (plural: *stelae*) – stone or wooden slab or column inscribed with commemorative texts.

tariqa – could mean either: 1) the spiritual path. 2) a mystic (Sufi) fellowship (order) with a spiritual lineage, descending from a **Pir**.

Tehuti – represents the Divine aspects of wisdom and intellect. It was **Tehuti** (Thoth) who uttered the words that created the world, as commanded by **Ra**. He is represented as the messenger of the **neteru** (gods/goddesses), of writing, language, and knowledge.

The Two Lands – represents the two earthly realms, where we exist in one, and each's twin of the opposite sex exists in the other. The two (twins) are subject to the same experiences from the date of birth to the date of death. In other words, the two represent the perfect mirror image. The concept of the Two Lands permeates Ancient Egyptian and present-day *Baladi* Egyptian traditions. [Read more in *Egyptian Cosmology: The Animated Universe*, by same author.]

truth – for the human being: the knowledge that the *I-ness* is not separate from the Whole.

Wali (plural: *awliya*) – used in various senses derived from its root-meaning of *nearness*, e.g. next of kin, patron, protector, friend, whose holiness brings them near to God, and who receive from Him, as tokens of His peculiar favor, miraculous gifts (**Ka-ra-ma-at**). The **Wali** therefore is a folk saint who the *Baladi* and Ancient Egyptians respect, visit, and ask favors. Unlike the saints in Christianity and Islamic Shiites, **Walis** in Egypt are chosen by ordinary people, based on performance. Once the people can see that this person does indeed have the ability to influence supernatural forces, in order to assist those on earth, and as a result fulfills their wishes, then he or she is considered to be a **Wali**. Also see **Pir**, **Mir**, and *mouled/moulid*.

zaffa – is an Egyptian term, which literally means *wedding procession*, for the purpose of consummating a marriage. The same term is used to describe the procession made to the shrine of the **Wali**, during his *mouled (s)*. The Egyptian term *zaffa* has a subtle reference to the unitive action—the inner marriage between the self (**Ka**—the personage of the **Wali**), and his soul (**Ba**).

zikr – a mystical practice intended to achieve *knowledge of God by way of revelations* in which states of visionary ecstasy are brought on by groups of purified mystic seekers, chanting of religious texts, rhythmic gestures, dancing, and deep breathing. [See Appendix C for details.]

Selected Bibliography

Ameen, Ahmed. *The Egyptian Customs, Traditions and Expressions.* Cairo, 1999 [Arabic text].

Arafa Abduh Ali. *The Mouleds of the Protected (Mahrosa) Egypt.* Cairo, 1995 [Arabic text].

Arberry, Arthur J. *Sufism: An Account of Mystics of Islam.* London, 1956.

Baldick, Julian. *Mystical Islam: An Introduction to Sufism.* New York and London, 1989.

Blackman, Aylward M. *Gods, Priests and Men: Studies in the Religion of Pharaonic Egypt.* London and New York, 1998.

Blackman, Winifred S. *The Fellahin of Upper Egypt.* London, 1968.

Bleeker, C.J. *Egyptian Festivals: Enactments of Religious Renewal.* Leiden, 1967.

Bleeker, C.J. *Hathor and Thoth.* Leiden, 1973.

Burke, O.M. *Among the Dervishes.* New York, 1975.

Catholic Encyclopedia, Online Edition, 1999. *http://www.newadvent.org/cathen/.*

El Hefni, Abd el-Menam. *The Sufi Dictionary.* Cairo, 1997 [Arabic text].

El-Beqli, Mohammed Qandeel. *(Egyptian) Dervishes Literature.* Cairo, 1970 [Arabic text].

Erman, Adolf. *Life in Ancient Egypt.* New York, 1971.

Fadiman, James & Robert Frager, editors. *Essential Sufism.* San Francisco, 1997.

Fahim, Shadia S. *Doris Lessing: Sufi Equilibrium and the Form of the Novel*. New York, 1994.

Farouk Ahmed Moustafa. *The Mouleds: A Study in the Popular Customs and Traditions in Egypt*. Alexandria, 1981 [Arabic text].

Gadalla, Moustafa. *Egyptian Cosmology: The Animated Universe*. USA, 2001.

Gadalla, Moustafa. *Egyptian Divinities: The All Who Are THE ONE*. USA, 2001.

Gadalla, Moustafa. *Egyptian Harmony: The Visual Music*. USA, 2000.

Gadalla, Moustafa. *Egyptian Rhythm: The Heavenly Melodies*. USA, 2002.

Gadalla, Moustafa. *Historical Deception: The Untold Story of Ancient Egypt – Second Edition*. USA, 1999.

Garnett, Lucy MJ. *Mysticism and Magic in Turkey*. London, 1912.

Gilsenan, Michael. *Saint and Sufi in Modern Egypt*. Oxford, 1973.

Greek Orthodox Archdiocese of America website. *www.goarch.org*. 2002.

Herodotus. *The Histories*. Tr. By Aubrey DeSelincourt. London, 1996.

Hoffman, Valerie J. *Sufism, Mystics and Saints in Modern Egypt*. Columbia, SC, USA, 1995.

Ibn-Arabi. *Sufis of Andalusia*. Tr. By RWJ Austin. Berkeley & LA, 1971.

Lane, Edward William. *An Account of the Manners and Customs of the Modern Egyptians*. New York, 1973.

Lifchez, Raymond. *The Dervish Lodge: Architecture, Art, and Sufism in Ottoman Turkey*. Berkeley (and L.A.), 1992.

McPherson, J.W. *The Moulids of Egypt (Egyptian Saints-Days)*. Cairo,

1941.

Nicholson, Reynold A. *The Mystics of Islam*. New York, 1975.

Pendlebury, David, Editor (Tr. From Arabic by Nabil Safwat, Compiled by Abd al-Razzaq al-Qashani). *A Glossary of Sufi Technical Terms*. London, 1991.

Piankoff, Alexandre. *The Litany of Re*. New York, 1964.

Piankoff, Alexandre. *Mythological Papyri*. New York, 1957.

Piankoff, Alexandre. *The Shrines of Tut-Ankh-Amon Texts*. New York, 1955.

Plato. *The Collected Dialogues of Plato including the Letters*. Edited by E. Hamilton & H. Cairns. New York, 1961.

Plutarch. *Plutarch's Moralia, Volume V*. Tr. by Frank Cole Babbitt. London, 1927.

Saleh, Ahmed Roshdi. *(Egyptian) Folk Literature*. Cairo, 1971 [Arabic text].

Shah, Idries. *The Sufis*. New York, 1964.

Sicilus, Diodorus. *Vol 1*. Tr. by C.H. Oldfather. London.

Subhan, John A. *Sufism: Its Saints and Shrines*. Lucknow [pref. 1938].

Trimingham, J. Spencer. *The Sufi Orders in Islam*. New York, 1998.

Waugh, Earle H. *The Munshidin of Egypt: Their World and Their Song*. Columbia, SC, USA, 1989.

Wilkinson, J. Gardner. *The Ancient Egyptians: Their Life and Customs*. London, 1988.

Other numerous Arabic texts.

Sources and Notes

The author is extremely knowledgeable of the Arabic language (his mother tongue) and Islam, being born-Moslem in Egypt and subjected to Islamic studies all his life.

References to sources in the previous section, *Selected Bibliography* are only referred to for the facts, events, and dates—not for their interpretations of such information.

Chapter 1 - Egyptian Mysticism and Islamized Sufism
Trimingham, Garnett, Shah (re. Dhu 'l-Nun and Tehuti).
Dhu 'l-Nun - Shah, Baldick, Arberry.
Old Religion - Shah, Arafa, Hoffman, Gadalla (being a native Egyptian).
Magical Powers of Egyptians - W. Blackman, Gadalla (being a native Egyptian), Shah.

Chapter 2 - The Treasure Within
Gadalla (*Egyptian Cosmology, Egyptian Divinities*), Fahim.
Organs of Perception - Fahim, Gadalla (*Egyptian Cosmology*).
Power of Love - practically all references.

Chapter 3 - The Alchemist Way
Atum/Adam - Gadalla (*Egyptian Cosmology*), Erman.
Mirror Metaphor - Gadalla (*Egyptian Cosmology*), Fahim, Shah.
Alchemy - Shah, Gadalla (*Egyptian Cosmology*).
Progressive Stages - Fadiman, Subhan, Trimingham, Hoffman.
Guides - Practically all references, especially Fadiman, Fahim,

Subhan, Gadalla (as a native Egyptian).

Thrice Tehuti - Shah, Nicholson, Gadalla (*Egyptian Cosmology, Egyptian Divinities*).

Chapter 4 - The Purification Process

Pure Gold - A. Blackman, Gadalla (*Egyptian Cosmology*), Bleeker (*Hathor*).

Healthy Body - A. Blackman, Shah, Gadalla (*Egyptian Cosmology*).

Out of Box - Gadalla (*Egyptian Cosmology*), Lifchez, Garnett, practically all references.

Enemies Within - Gadalla (*Egyptian Cosmology*).

The Ego - Gadalla (*Egyptian Cosmology*), Austin, Nicholson, Fadiman.

Self-development - Lifchez, Waugh, Hoffman, Subhan, Arafa.

Chapter 5 - Basic Practices

Concentration, Breathing, and Music - Gadalla (*Egyptian Rhythm*), Hoffman, Fahim, Garnett.

Recitation of Names and Rosaries - Hoffman, Waugh, Ameen, Arafa, Gilsenan, McPherson, Gadalla (*Egyptian Cosmology, Historical Deception*), Bleeker (*Festivals*).

Sports - Diodorus, Gadalla (*Exiled Egyptians*).

Games - McPherson, Wilkinson.

Contemplating Death - Ameen.

Zikr - Arafa, Subhan, Farouk, Gilsenan.

Enduring Love - McPherson.

Chapter 6 - The Way to Revelations

Ra - Gadalla (*Egyptian Cosmology*), Piankoff (*Litany of Re*).

Dualities - Gadalla (*Egyptian Cosmology*) and practically all references.

Reconciliation of Dualities - Gadalla (*Egyptian Cosmology*), and practically all references.

Zikr - Burke, Arafa, Waugh, Hoffman, Farouk, McPherson, Lane, Fadiman, Gilsenan (high marks for his book), Nicholson, Subhan, Austin, W. Blackman, Gadalla (being a native Egyptian).

Unification and Deification (Pir) - Gadalla (*Egyptian Cosmology*), Nicholson, Arafa, Fadiman, Subhan.

Chapter 7 - The Heavenly Helpers
Perfect Servants - Nicholson, Subhan, Wilkinson.
Staying Alive - Lifchez, W. Blackman, A. Blackman, Lane, Subhan.
Shrines - Gadalla (*Egyptian Cosmology*), Arafa, Lifchez, Lane, Erman.

Chapter 8 - The Cyclical Renewal Festivals
Renewal Need - Bleeker (*Festivals*), Arafa.
Mouleds History - Bleeker (*Festivals*), W. Blackman, Lane.
Festival Regulators - Diodorus, Plutarch.
Setting the Dates - Gadalla, Plutarch, Wilkinson, Diodorus, McPherson, Lane, Herodotus, *Catholic Encyclopedia*, Greek Orthodox website.

Chapter 9 - Samples of Ancient-Present Festivals
Gadalla, Catholic Encyclopedia, Greek Orthodox website, McPherson, Wilkinson, Lane, Plutarch, Ameen, Diodorus.
Annual Jubilee of Egyptian King - Bleeker (*Festivals*), A. Blackman, Erman.
Latin New Year's Day - A. Blackman.

Chapter 10 - The Egyptian Spirited Fairs (Mouleds)
Now - McPherson, Arafa, Waugh, W. Blackman, Lane, Ameen, Gadalla (as a native Egyptian).
Ancient Egypt - Bleeker (*Festivals*), W. Blackman, Wilkinson, Gadalla (*Egyptian Divinities*).

Chapter 11 - Fellowship Formations
Universality of Egyptian Mysticism - Garnett, Fadiman, Fahim, Hoffman (re. women), Gadalla (*Egyptian Cosmology*).
Fellowship Elements - Lifchez, Garnett, Lane, McPherson, Gilsenan, Hoffman, Subhan, Arafa, Waugh, Lifchez, Egyptian (Arabic) references.

Chapter 12 - Auset (Isis) -The Model Philosopher
Gadalla (*Egyptian Cosmology*), Plutarch.

Appendix A - Sufi Terms
1. Gazelle - Bleeker (*Festivals*).
2. Music of Stones - Fahim, Gadalla (*Egyptian Rhythm*), Shah.
3. Word of God - Gadalla (*Egyptian Cosmology, Egyptian Divinities*).
4. Names of God - Gadalla (*Egyptian Cosmology*).
5. Writing, Sacred Geometry, etc - Fahim, Gadalla (*Egyptian Harmony, Egyptian Rhythm*), Shah, Plato.
6. Heart and Tongue - Gadalla (*Egyptian Cosmology*).
7. Canopus Doctrine - Bleeker (*Egyptian Festivals*), Shah, Gadalla (*Egyptian Divinities*).
8. Fountain of Youth and El Khidr - Lane, Subhan, Garnett, McPherson, Shah, Gadalla (*Egyptian Cosmology, Egyptian Divinities*).

Apendix B - Sleeping With the Enemy
Gadalla (being a native Egyptian), Arafa, Bell, Subhan, Shah, Hoffman.

Appendix C - Zikr
Burke, Arafa, Waugh, Hoffman, Farouk, McPherson, Lane, Fadiman, Gilsenan, Nicholson, Subhan, Austin, W. Blackman, Gadalla (being a native Egyptian).

Appendix D - Reaching Hearts and Minds (Effective Communication)
Gadalla (*Egyptian Cosmology*), Fahim, Saleh, el-Baqli.

Appendix E - Egyptian and Latin Calendars
Gadalla (*Egyptian Cosmology, Egyptian Rhythm*), Wilkinson, McPherson, Lane.

Index

About TRF Books

Tehuti Research Foundation (T.R.F.) is a non-profit, international organization, dedicated to Ancient Egyptian studies. Our books are engaging, factual, well researched, practical, interesting, and appealing to the general public. Visit our website at:

http://www.egypt-tehuti.org
E-mail address: info@egypt-tehuti.org
eBooks can be ordered at: http://www.egypt-tehuti.org/gadalla-books.html

The books listed below are authored by T.R.F. chairman, Moustafa Gadalla.

Egyptian Cosmology: The Animated Universe - 2ⁿᵈ ed.

ISBN: 0-9652509-3-8 (pbk.), 192 pages, US$11.95
eBook: 1-931446-03-2, 192 pages, US$7.95

Discover the Egyptian concept of monotheism, number mysticism, the universal energy matrix, how the social and political structures were a reflection of the universe, and the interactions between the nine universal realms, ...etc. The book surveys the applicability of Egyptian concepts to our modern understanding of the nature of the universe, creation, science, and philosophy. Egyptian cosmology is the ONLY metaphysics of all (ancient and modern) that is coherent, comprehensive, consistent, logical, analytical, and rational.

Egyptian Divinities: The All Who Are THE ONE

ISBN: 1-931446-04-0 (pbk.), 128 pages, US$ 8.95
eBook: 1-931446-07-5, 128 pages, US$5.95

The Egyptian concept of God is based on recognizing the multiple attributes (gods/goddesses) of the Divine. Far from being a primitive, polytheistic concept, the Egyptian Way is the highest expression of monotheistic mysticism. The book details more than 80 divinities (gods/goddesses), how they act and interact to maintain the universe, and how they operate in the human being—*As Above so Below, and As Below so Above.*

Egyptian Harmony: The Visual Music
ISBN: 0-9652509-8-9 (pbk.), 192 pages, US$11.95
eBook: 1-931446-08-3, 192 pages, US$7.95

This book reveals the Ancient Egyptian incredible and comprehensive knowledge of harmonic proportion, sacred geometry, and number mysticism, as manifested in their texts, temples, tombs, ...etc., throughout their known history. Discover how the Word (sound) that created the World (forms) was likewise transformed to visual music by the Egyptians into hieroglyphs, art, and architecture. The book surveys the Ancient Egyptian harmonic proportional application in all aspects of their civilization.

Historical Deception
The Untold Story of Ancient Egypt - 2nd Edition
ISBN: 0-9652509-2-X (pbk.), 352 pages, US$19.95
eBook: 1-931446-09-1, 352 pages, US$13.95

This book reveals the ingrained prejudices against Ancient Egypt, from religious groups, who deny that Egypt is the source of their creed, and Western academicians, who deny the existence of science and philosophy prior to the Greeks. The book contains 46 chapters, with many interesting topics, such as the Egyptian medical knowledge about determining the sex of the unborn, and much, much more.

Exiled Egyptians: The Heart of Africa
ISBN: 0-9652509-6-2 (pbk.), 352 pages, US$19.95
eBook: 1-931446-10-5, 352 pages, US13.95

Read about the forgotten Ancient Egyptians, who fled the foreign invasions and religious oppressors. Read how they rebuilt the Ancient Egyptians model system in Africa, when Egypt itself became an Arab colony. Find out how the Islamic jihads fragmented and dispersed the African continent into endless misery and chaos. Read about the superiority of the Ancient Egyptians' social, economical, and political systems, and their extended application into sub-Sahara Africa. This book uncovers the chaotic state of Western academia on the subjects of Ancient Egypt and Africa.

Pyramid Handbook - Second Edition
ISBN: 0-9652509-4-6 (pbk.), 192 pages, US$11.95
eBook: 1-931446-11-3, 192 pages, US$7.95

A complete handbook about the pyramids of Ancient Egypt during the Pyramid Age. It contains: the locations and dimensions of interiors and exteriors of the pyramids; the history and builders of the pyramids; theories of construction; theories on their purpose and function; the sacred geometry that was incorporated into the design of the pyramids; and much, much more.

Tut-Ankh-Amen: The Living Image of the Lord
ISBN: 0-9652509-9-7 (pbk.), 144 pages, US$9.50
eBook: 1-931446-12-1, 144 pages, US$6.50

This book provides the overwhelming evidence from archeology, the Dead Sea Scrolls, the Talmud, and the Bible itself, that Tut-Ankh-Amen was the historical character of Jesus. The book examines the details of Tut's birth, life, death, resurrection, family roots, religion, teachings, etc., which were duplicated in the biblical account of Jesus.

Egypt: A Practical Guide
ISBN: 0-9652509-3-0 (pbk.), 256 pages, US$8.50
eBook: 1-931446-13-X, 256 pages, US$5.95

A no-nonsense, no-clutter, practical guide to Egypt, written by an Egyptian-American Egyptologist. Quick, easy, and comprehensive reference to sites of antiquities and recreation. Find your way with numerous maps and illustrations.

Egyptian Rhythm: The Heavenly Melodies
ISBN: 1-931446-02-4 (pbk.), 240 pages, US$14.95
eBook: 1-931446-14-8, 240 pages, US$9.95

Discover the cosmic roots of Egyptian musical, vocal, and dancing rhythmic forms. Learn the fundamentals (theory and practice) of music in the typical Egyptian way. Review a detailed description of the major Egyptian musical instruments, playing techniques, functions, etc. Discover the Egyptian rhythmic practices in all aspects of their lives.

Tehuti Research Foundation
Ordering Information (Paperback Books)

Name _____

Address _____

City _____

State/Province _____

Country _____Tel. (_____) _____

_____ books @ $11.95 (*Egyptian Mystics*)   = $

_____ books @ $11.95 (*Egyptian Cosmology*)   = $

_____ books @ $ 8.95 (*Egyptian Divinities*)   = $

_____ books @ $11.95 (*Egyptian Harmony*)   = $

_____ books @ $19.95 (*Historical Deception*)   = $

_____ books @ $19.95 (*Exiled Egyptians*)   = $

_____ books @ $11.95 (*Pyramid Handbook*)   = $

_____ books @ $ 9.50 (*Tut-Ankh-Amen*)   = $

_____ books @ $ 8.50 (*Egypt: Pract. Guide*)   = $

_____ books @ $14.95 (*Egyptian Rhythm*)   = $_____

                                        Subtotal   = $

North Carolina residents, add 7% Sales Tax   = $

Shipping: (U.S.A. only) $1.00 each book   = $

Outside U.S.A. (per weight/destination)   = $_____

                                        Total   = $

Payment: [ ] Money Order or Check
          [ ] Visa   [ ] MasterCard   [ ] Discover

Card Number: _____

Name on Card: _____ Exp. Date: ____/____

Tehuti Research Foundation
P.O. Box 39406
Greensboro, NC   27438-9406   U.S.A.

Call TOLL FREE (N. America) and order now 888-826-7021
Call to order (Outside N. America) 336-855-8111
Fax (N. America): 888-202-7818 (Outside N.A.): 775-402-0867
e-mail: info@egypt-tehuti.org